CITY, RICE-SWAMP, AND HILL

CITY, RICE-SWAMP, AND HILL

W. JOHNSON

GYAN

Published by

Gyan Publishing House
5, Ansari Road
Daryaganj, New Delhi-110002
Phone: 011-47034999, 9811692060
E-mail: books@gyanbooks.com

Distribution Network
gyanbooks.com
India, USA, Canada, UK, Australia

ISBN: 978-93-7169-640-1 (PB)

First Published, 1893

2nd Impression 2025

Printed at: Gyan Press, Delhi.

CITY, RICE-SWAMP, AND HILL
Author: W. JOHNSON

THE BHOWANIPUR INSTITUTION.

CITY, RICE-SWAMP, AND HILL.

BY

W. JOHNSON, B.A.,

MISSIONARY OF THE LONDON MISSIONARY SOCIETY IN CALCUTTA
FOR THIRTY-ONE YEARS.

1893.

PREFACE.

JOHN SMEATON, the engineer, having retired from his profession, determined to devote "his remaining time to the description of the several works performed under his direction." His literary work went on slowly, and with growing dissatisfaction to himself. In his "Narrative of the Construction of the Eddystone Lighthouse," he says: "I have found much more difficulty in writing than I did in building." He was "employed full seven years, at every opportunity," in preparing his narrative. The building itself was despatched in less than half that time.

The writing of this little book was begun through the suggestion and advice of a missionary friend with whom I lived and worked in happy relationship for about twenty years. I can sympathise with the feelings of the engineer when he had turned author. There would be less difficulty and more satisfaction to me in doing missionary work than in writing about it.

So far as I have dealt with scenes and events remote from the time, sphere, and experiences of my own missionary work, I have necessarily availed myself of what others have recorded. My indebtedness, however, is indicated in the text, though I have refrained from mentioning names in many cases.

I desire here to express my grateful affection for the men and women with whom I was associated in counsel, work, and prayer, both those who are still toiling in this valley below and those who are now rejoicing before the throne on high.

WILLIAM JOHNSON.

41, PARK VIEW, MANNINGHAM,
BRADFORD, *May*, 1893.

CONTENTS.

CITY, RICE-SWAMP, AND HILL.

CHAPTER I.

OUR INDIAN COSMOS AND ITS RIGHTFUL LORD.

LORD DUFFERIN, just before he left India, made a great speech, in which he drew a striking picture of our Eastern Empire. He touched on the numerous races, the distinct nationalities, the many languages, the differing religions, the various stages of civilisation —all of which go to make up our Indian world. The census report, he remarked, gives one hundred and six distinct Indian tongues. Besides the peoples who are directly under our rule, the British Government has to exercise a certain amount of supervision over one hundred and seventeen native states. He had a passing word for "the intelligent traveller who has come to India for three months with the intention of writing an encyclopædic work on its government and people, and who is therefore able to speak in a spirit of infallibility denied to us lesser men." His aim was to give an idea of the greatness and difficulty of the work of governing this congeries of nations. The friends of missions have to remember that the Church's problem in India corresponds to the political problem in vastness, complexity, and difficulty. We "have need of patience."

What is this Indian Empire? It is equal in extent to the Continent of Europe, if Russia be excepted. The last census shows a population of 280 millions. "Perhaps the most patent peculiarity of our Indian Cosmos is its division into two mighty political communities—the Hindus, numbering 200 millions, and the Muhammadans, 50 millions." These communities contain nationalities as distinct and different from each other in race, language, customs, character, as are the nations of Europe. There are warlike peoples on our frontiers. There are many tribes of "hill-men dwelling in the folds of the Himalayas." There are about ten millions in Burmah who have been recently added to the subjects of the British Government, Mongolians in race, Buddhists in religion.

And what is India with regard to civilisation? In England, as a whole, we have reached a civilisation in the advantages of which all classes of the community share. In India, at one and the same time, are existing all the stages of civilisation through which mankind has passed from the earliest ages to the present day. "At one end of the scale we have the naked savage hill-man, with his stone weapons, his head hunting, his polyandrous habits, his childish superstitions; and at the other end, the Europeanised native gentleman, with his refinement and polish, his literary culture, his western philosophy, and his advanced political ideas." Between these extremes are "wandering communities, with their flocks of goats and moving tents; collections of undisciplined warriors, with their blood feuds, their clan organisation, and loose tribal government; feudal chiefs and barons, with their picturesque retainers, and their mediæval modes of life; modernised country gentlemen and enterprising merchants and manufacturers, with their well-managed estates and prosperous enterprises." So much for the India that is visible. There is also an invisible India, of hoary superstitions and errors, of deep prejudices, of ancient traditions, of long-transmitted antipathies. Into this deeper and darker India the missionary has to descend, to familiarise himself with it, and there to "wrestle against principalities, against powers, against the rulers of the darkness of this world, against spiritual wickedness in high places."

What is the power and what are the prospects of Christianity in India? The impressions of visitors are sometimes in strong contrast to the opinions of men of a long Indian experience. Some, even Christian men, have visited the country, and declared that the task of converting India to Christianity seems hopeless. It is not difficult to understand such an impression. The visitor to North India, let us say, is struck with the sight of thronging multitudes in the great cities. He sees scores of thousands absorbed in the celebration of their religious festivals. Let a man stand on a housetop in the city of Benares, and look down on eighty thousand people celebrating the Ram Lila in honour of their favourite hero and god, Rama. The drama enacted along the streets represents the hero's return from exile, a joyous and touching event in the legend of Rama. How interested the multitudes are as they go forth to welcome back the long-banished, unhappy, but virtuous prince! The spectator will feel how dear these old legends are to the hearts of the people. Day by day he will see the sacred river alive with men and women standing up to the middle in the water, worshipping, and washing away their sins. He will meet crowds of pilgrims

CHRISTIAN LYRIC BAND, TRAVANCORE.

on their way to holy shrines. The temples are thronged. Then truly may he feel oppressed with the power of Hinduism. It fills the air. It is seen and heard all around. It sweeps on in its might, self-absorbed, self-sufficient, disdaining, or not noticing, aught but itself. In such scenes, how weak seems the power, how poor the prospects, of Christianity! How few, in comparison, its adherents! Where are they?

What is it against this resistless tide? So, even a Christian visitor might come back to England with the impression that the conversion of India is a hopeless task.

Side by side with this, place the opinions of men whose long experience and high position in the country were a guarantee that they knew the land and people well. A late Lieutenant-Governor of the Punjab and member of the Governor-General's Council writes thus: "The changes that are to-day being wrought out by Christian missionaries are marvellous. Teaching wherever they go the universal brotherhood of man, and animated by a faith which goes beyond the ties of caste or family relationship, Christian missionaries are slowly, but none the less surely, undermining the foundations of heathen superstition, and bringing about a peaceful, religious, moral and social revolution." A Government report published a few years ago in Calcutta declared that "native Christians were the most progressive class of the community." A Governor-General testified to the influence of Christian teachers when he said that missionaries had done more than had been effected by all the measures passed by Government to conciliate native feeling to British rule.

Are the natives of India receiving Christianity? There is success *and* success. In some parts of the land there has been an abundance of the success we all wish to see—the ingathering of great numbers. In other parts such results have been very meagre. In the extreme south of India, about thirteen hundred miles from my own station, I saw one of the most fruitful garden spots in the empire. I came upon a mission station very early one morning, after spending the night in a bullock-cart. Now, to pass the night in a bullock-cart without springs, travelling along roads with deep ruts, is conducive to the habit of early rising. So I had walked some miles when, at dawn, I reached the mission bungalow. It was in a lonely but beautiful spot, and commanded a view of distant green hills and a wide plain covered with forests of palms and other trees of varied foliage. After a bath and breakfast, I talked with my missionary brother about his work. He had fourteen thousand native Christians in his charge, and directed the work of about one hundred and thirty agents. "And within a year or two," said he, "I could make them twenty thousand, if I had a little money to enable me to place preachers and pastors among them. If you will stay with me a day or two, I will take you to five villages of which the people are all ready to come over if I give them the least encouragement." Here and elsewhere I found missionaries reluctant to swell the number of adherents because they were unable to place pastors and teachers among them.

The sight which most filled me with joy and hope was reserved for a Sunday morning. I entered the pulpit of the large church at the principal station, and saw before me a congregation of about nine hundred people. How much did I wish that some of our friends in England and elsewhere could have stood where I was! What a sight it was! The women especially I noticed. Along the roads, and in the villages, I had seen heathen women of the same class, and they looked so poor, melancholy, pinched, clothed only from the waist downwards, according to heathen custom, which regarded them as little better than beasts. These Christian women looked so raised above all that, so clean, becomingly dressed, satisfied, some of them decent-looking matrons with large Bibles open before them. In this nest of missions, connected with the London Missionary Society, there were then more than forty thousand adherents.

At the close of this visit I had to catch a train to travel northwards. By accident I got a glimpse of another prosperous mission. The railway was fifty miles from the mission station. My conveyance was a bullock-cart again. The rate of travelling varied from 0 to 3 miles an hour. The latter may be regarded as full speed. I started about nine o'clock p.m. The train was to leave about noon next day. The driver fell asleep. The bullocks fell asleep. The passenger also slept. I am not sure we were not moving even then. In India they are experts in somnambulism. But we were not going full speed. At times I awoke and shouted: "Come up." The driver awoke and shouted: "Come up." The bullocks, as requested, came up. So we moved more quickly at lucid intervals. But I reached Tinnivelli too late for the train. The native station-master advised me to wait for the next train, which would leave in about eighteen hours. I was glad of the opportunity of calling on the Venerable Bishop Sargent, of the C.M.S. We went into the church near his house, and he said: "We have on Sundays a congregation here of about eleven hundred people." He invited me to accompany him and a party of friends to the opening services at a new church, which had been built to accommodate a congregation of two thousand people.

In 1881 there were 95,624 adherents in the missions of the Church of England in Tinnivelli. These missions of the C.M.S. and S.P.G. lie out of the route of visitors to the famous cities and scenes of India, but the Christian traveller would be cheered and rewarded if he could turn aside to see them.

When we pass from the extreme south to the north of the country, we feel that we are on a harder mission field. Numerical results are meagre in comparison. Christian communities are small. Increase is slow. I am referring to educated and caste people on the great northern plains. In the statistics published by the London Mission, it is instructive to notice how numbers diminish as we pass from the extreme south to the north. The Society divides its Indian work into three fields—Travancore, South India, North India. In the first of these the total number of adherents is about 50,000. In the second it is 10,000. In the last it is only 2,543. Yet the number of English missionaries in North India has commonly been twice as large as that in Travancore, and it is the Society's oldest mission in the country. The experience of other Societies is much the same.

Missionaries have been asked: "Why do you not show in the North such results as we see in the South?" The question is natural. The answer is obvious. The conditions are different. Why is it not so easy to cut figures in stone as to mould them in wax? Why is not marble as pliant as clay? Why can we not drive a plough over the surface of a rock with the same results as through a deep yielding soil? It has been said: "Change your methods thus and thus, and you shall see the successes of Tinnivelli

THE MAHARAJAH'S COLLEGE, TRAVANCORE.

and Travancore repeated among the educated and high-caste Hindus elsewhere." I do not think that any one acquainted with the populations in question would, after due consideration, venture to make such a promise. But the North has its encouragements. They are not so striking as those of the South, yet they bear in them the seeds of a still greater triumph for the nations of India. We see "the mighty stream of tendency" moving towards a better day. We see the moulding influence of Christianity even where it is not acknowledged. We see, too, in the ever-growing Christian community that steady progress from decade to decade which means conquest. I shall quote a statement made by Sir W. W. Hunter, in an address he read a few years ago before the Society of Arts in London. This gentleman lived many years in India, and superintended the Indian census. He said: "The official census, notwithstanding its obscurities of classification . . . attests the rapid increase of the Christian population. So far as any inference for British India can be deduced, the normal rate of increase among the general population was 8 per cent., while the actual rate of increase of the Christian population was over 30 per cent." His statements regarding the great province of Bengal, which contains one-third of the whole population of British India, are of special interest. He shows that in the nine years preceding 1881, the general population increased at the rate of about 11 per cent.; the Muhammadans at about the same rate; the Hindus at about 13 per cent., and the native Christians at the rate of 64 per cent. "My acquaintance with the causes underlying the increase of populations, and with the science of gauging increase, would prevent me from accepting this enormous increase of 64 per cent. in nine years as ground for believing that a similar increase will take place during the next ten years. All I can say is this, that if the native Christian population is increasing 64 per cent. during these ten years, it will be one of the most wonderful triumphs which Christianity has ever had in the world."

The rapid progress I have referred to, in the South, has been made among non-caste peoples. They were the drudges and slaves of Hinduism, trodden under its feet, not recognised as within its community, below the lowest caste. They were forbidden even to appear in the market-places, and did not dare to meet a caste man on the roads. An incident of my visit to the South brought this sharply before me. As I was walking with a friend, we saw a number of men coming towards us. They turned aside into the jungle, and stood behind trees until we had gone by. My friend's horse and trap were behind us with his servant. "Why did those men get behind the trees?" I asked. "That was on account of my horse-keeper," he said. "He would have been defiled to meet them. If they had dared to pass him on the road, he might have horsewhipped them —if I had not been here." The missionary has gone among people extremely poor, oppressed, helpless; and he has set himself to get them recognised as men, with human rights. They have had nothing to lose and everything to gain by submitting to Christianity; and they have yielded plentiful harvests to the Christian labourer.

Missionary successes among aboriginal and non-caste peoples show how much more ready they are to receive the Gospel than the old caste-ridden Hindu races. Throughout India the original tribes, the low-castes, and the out-castes, furnish at the least four-fifths of all the converts gained to Christianity. It is needful to remember that prosperity in these directions commonly makes fresh and larger demands on the Christian Church. The tendency with us is, when a mission has proved itself prosperous, to leave it to take care of itself. We expect to be relieved of demands. But the nature of the prosperity must be considered. Success may increase rather than diminish our responsibilities. This is the case when it means, not that intelligent people have embraced Christianity on a conviction of its truth, but that masses of extremely ignorant and poor people have put themselves under Christian teaching, feeling it will somehow be better for them. Such an event is indeed very far from what we understand by the soul's conversion to Christ. And a missionary might well hesitate to speak of a great accession of such adherents as so many thousands converted to the Lord. But surely it is a matter of joy and thankfulness, and a ground for far-reaching hopes, when tribes of people, humble and docile, though ignorant and superstitious, come to the missionary and say: "We will accept you as our teacher. We will be Christians and no longer worship our idols." It is a great matter when we can form them into congregations, and establish schools among them. If we are ready at any sacrifice to preach the Gospel to them, doubly should we be concerned, when they are won, that Christ should be formed in them, that character, life, society, should become purified and elevated. For the fruit of labour is lost, unless people who have consented to come under the Christian name are taught what the Christian religion is, and what a Christian life is. Years ago, I heard missionaries express fears of being swamped by masses of ignorance for which they could provide no adequate instruction. Even now we read of missionaries in the Madras Presidency holding back from fields that seem ripe unto the harvest, because they have no helpers to send to the reaping.

CHAPTER II.

A SUBURB OF THE GREAT CITY.

BHOWANIPUR, the city of the goddess Bhowani, is the central station of the London Missionary Society's work in Bengal. Of the four suburbs which form the southern boundary of Calcutta, Bhowanipur is the largest. It is not a pretty green rural suburb, as my fancy painted it, while on my way to India, but a thickly peopled and almost purely native quarter. The main road, which lies north and south between the city and Bhowanipur, is the finest in Calcutta. On the eastern side it is "bordered with the stately mansions of the English, with their white walls, broad open verandahs, and green venetian shutters." From these mansions Calcutta gets its name, "The City of Palaces." On the other side it is lined for a mile and a half with a beautiful grassy plain, called "The Maidan," which reaches westward to the very edge of the river. Refreshing breezes from the water play freely over its surface, and to get into the centre of it away from the dust and heat of the neighbouring streets, feels like getting out upon the breezy ocean, so fresh is it. It is green all the year round, and its beauty is enhanced by clusters of trees dotted over its surface; while here and there are majestic old specimens standing alone, silent, venerable, casting a mighty and kindly shade. I have felt grateful to the men who long ago planted these stately trees, that others might look on their beauty and enjoy their shelter. Near the southern extremity of the plain is the handsome cathedral built by Bishop Wilson, with the hope, it would seem, that so imposing an expression of our religion would impress Hindus in favour of Christianity. I know no evidence that such a result has come about, whatever other good ends have been answered. Opposite, stands the Bishop's Palace. Behind the cathedral, stretching across the plain, is a fine long avenue of trees. Often have I walked to and fro, or sat and read under them, and looked out upon the dazzling atmosphere, tremulous with burning heat. In India we know the meaning of 'a shadow in a weary land.'

A little more to the south, we cross the boundary road of the city, the Mahratta ditch, and are in Bhowanipur. Here, the clean, the beautiful, the stately, ends; dirt and squalor begin. I describe it as it was not many years ago. The road is ankle-deep in dust. Dust clouds, raised by constant traffic, fill the air. The passengers in a vehicle are bumped and jolted into hollows and over ridges. It is a journey of sudden shocks and deep groans. An abominable open drain runs alongside the footpath, a bed of liquid typhoid. The shops in the native bazar are sheds without windows. Piles of sweetmeats are exposed, unprotected from dust, with swarms of wasps and fat flies buzzing about them.

Bah! how strong is the smell of rancid fat! Here a money-changer sits on a platform, tailor-wise and almost naked, amid little piles of dirty copper coins and cowries. Another establishment is a collection of odds and ends, pieces of English crockery, a few glass tumblers, some oil lamps, old spoons and knives, the whole stock-in-trade probably not worth half a crown. How does the man manage to make a living out of them? The workers in silver and brass, the blacksmith with his bellows and anvil, tailors, shoemakers, are all to be seen in their frontless shops, sitting on the ground, with the implements and materials of their trade about them. The silversmith works behind an iron grating for protection. Grog-shops, alas! are numerous. The rum-seller squats aloft on the beams that support his spirit-casks, waiting, like an evil bird, for his prey. The grain-shops, with many varieties of cereals, are pleasant to look upon. They remind one of Nature and of golden harvest fields, and are a happy contrast to the grog-shops.

The traveller southward along this busy, dusty road cannot fail to notice the large, handsome building on the left, with an inscription on its front, "*The London Missionary Society's Institution.*" It has a noble appearance, and occupies a commanding position, with library, lecture-rooms, and class-rooms; it contains accommodation for 1,100 scholars.

Near the college was built a house for Christian converts, really a house of refuge to meet hard necessities. A Christian life in a Hindu home was, except in rare cases, an impossibility. Hence a shelter had to be provided for young converts.

There have been happy exceptions to this impossibility. A Bengali gentleman of Calcutta, at present one of the best known and most influential members of the native Christian community, was at the time of his conversion the head of his family, though only a young man. He remained in his home, being master there. The relaxing of caste will ere long, it is to be hoped, allow converts to stay with their friends. I have heard young men in the refuge praying tenderly for the dear ones they had left: "those who are mourning and lamenting for us as lost, may they be comforted and enlightened!"

South of the institution, lying well back from the main road, is the first mission house built in the station. It is relieved from the noise and dust of the thoroughfare by a line of trees and a garden. The house was erected as a residence for the missionary in charge of the institution. Changes in European life are rapid in India. The tenure of houses is brief. A long succession of occupants that house has known since it was built, less than forty years ago. To my knowledge seven mission families have resided there, besides four unmarried missionaries. Some were compelled to remove through failing health. Some passed from that house to the presence of their Lord. I have seen young men struck down after a few months in the country, and older men called away after the service of a quarter of a century. Yet during thirty years of missionary life in India, that house was my only home.

A prominent object in the station is the large Zenana home, built a few years ago. Altogether this Christian settlement, with its college for boys and young men, its house for converts, its day and boarding schools for girls, its home for Zenana missionaries and their assistants, its mission houses, its garden plots and shady trees, is an extensive and complete station. To me, entering the peaceful enclosure after journeyings from home, it seemed an oasis in the desert. It is a busy hive of Christian workers. In its schools and homes, a thousand human beings, many a day, would be assembled.

A mile and a half farther south is a celebrated temple of the goddess Kali, peculiarly sacred, and visited from many and remote parts of India. We see companies of pilgrims on their way to the temple, flocks of goats being driven for sacrifice, the devotee measuring his length on the ground to the presence of the awful deity. There is the modern convenience of trams, which are freely used by all classes of the people. Hundreds of men, almost all clerks, go by tram every morning to the city, and, in the cool of the evening, walk back home over the grassy "maidan." It is curious to notice in India the ancient superstitions in juxtaposition with modern civilisation. The trams bring many worshippers to the temple of Kali. Pilgrims avail themselves of railways to perform their religious journeys to holy shrines. The water of the sacred Ganges is sent hundreds of miles by rail to bathe some ancient idol.

The neighbourhood of Bhowanipur abounds in Brahmanical families. In quiet lanes, off the noisy, dusty thoroughfare, are large family mansions of the native gentry. These great houses stand often amid miserable surroundings. To native men of wealth, beautiful environments for their houses are

THE MONKEY TEMPLE, BENARES.

not a felt necessity. In the great city itself, many houses, palaces in appearance and size, are in mean and filthy neighbourhoods. Scarcely could one think that this thickly peopled and dirty quarter was at one time selected by wealthy Europeans as a pleasant site for garden-houses. So it was, however. Opposite our college was an extensive, neglected garden called "Foster's Folly." In the midst of a fine pond stood a round summer-house. The fish in the pond were treated with great consideration, no one being allowed to catch or molest them. They were so tame that they came to the very steps of the ghat to be fed with rice, and so fat they seemed to have difficulty in moving their tails to steer themselves to take the offerings. A visit to "Foster's Folly," with an offering for the fat fish, was a great treat to my little boys.

There is an interesting house in the grounds adjoining our mission station—the house built by the first Protestant missionary to Northern India, John Kiernander, a native of Sweden. Kiernander came to Calcutta thirty-five years before the arrival of Carey. He had been settled at Cuddalore in South India since 1740, and, when that place surrendered to the French, and the Protestant mission was broken up, he had to direct his thoughts to other fields of missionary enterprise. He was invited by Clive "to plant the cross in Bengal, and in 1758 he left the pleasant sea-breezes of Cuddalore for the dust-charged atmosphere of Calcutta." By a second marriage he became a wealthy man, and besides using much of his wealth for Christian ends, he built for himself a large and substantial garden-house at Bhowanipur. In this house and its large compound the work of our mission was carried on for years.

Bhowanipur was chosen as the site of a permanent mission in 1837. The situation was well chosen. In the neighbourhood was a population of about forty thousand. It was determined to open, at this southern extremity of Calcutta, an English day school for Hindu and Muhammadan boys on the model of the institution which had been so successful under Dr. Duff at the northern extremity of the city, five miles distant.

Dr. Duff began his institution in July, 1830, with five pupils. By the end of the same week there were more than three hundred applicants for admission. Nine years after, the five who entered on the day of its commencement had swollen into an average attendance of eight hundred.

Six Hindu youths entered our little school at Bhowanipur on the day it was opened in 1837; "a small instalment of the many thousands that have since followed." The building stood in a corner of the garden belonging to Kiernander's old residence. The school grew rapidly, and the bungalow was enlarged. In five years the six scholars had increased to three hundred and fifty, the number in 1843. In that year the baptism of three students so alarmed the Hindu community that the numbers fell at once to one hundred and fifty. Gradually, however, the scholars returned; two branch schools were established at Behala, a large Brahman village, four miles to the south-west of Bhowanipur, and at Ballygunge, two miles to the eastward. At the close of 1850, a few months before the laying of the foundation stone of the large building now used, the institution and the two branch schools contained eight hundred and twenty scholars.

The 2nd of February, 1854, was a day of joy and thankfulness to our missionaries in Calcutta. On that day the friends of the London Missionary Society met for the first time in the stately building for which the humble school bungalow in Kiernander's garden had been discarded. This meeting closed a series of interesting services by which the new establishment was formally opened. Sermons had been preached in our two English chapels. At a special meeting for prayer, the institution had been commended to God, and the Divine blessing sought on its work among the young.

The cost of all the buildings erected to give completeness to the educational establishment was six thousand eight hundred pounds. Dr. Boaz, while on a lengthened visit to England, excited a warm interest in the work, and gathered for it a large sum of money. Indeed, the institution is a noble monument to his memory.

For seventeen years the work had been carried on in an unpretentious, inexpensive building. But that earlier period illustrates the truth that the efficiency of a mission does not depend on costly erections. It is often by inferior means that God accomplishes great ends. There are still living, in Calcutta and other parts of North India, elderly members of our native church, who well remember the mental stir and the awakening of young hearts in those earlier days, and whose conversion dates from that period. It was a time when souls were won for Christ; when the entrance of the truth carried divisions, bitterness, and anguish into Hindu homes; when, through the intolerance of caste, fathers and children were parted for life; when such hopes as gather round an only son were blighted; when loss and sacrifice were willingly accepted for Christ's sake; when the Hindu community became alarmed by these innovations, and the truth was opposed with bitterness, sometimes even with raging violence.

Four well-known missionaries of Calcutta arranged to give a course of lectures in English on Christianity. These were Dr. Duff, the originator of the new movement, Archdeacon Daltry, Mr. Hill, and Mr. Adam, the latter two of the London Mission. The lectures were attended by a large number of native gentlemen, mostly students, and produced great excitement. The attack was a surprise. Western ideas combined with Christian teaching, and presented in the English tongue, which all were eager to learn, —here was a new and dangerous weapon to be used against Hinduism. One who witnessed the effect declared that the whole town was in an uproar.

"Two native newspapers were then published in Calcutta, in Bengali. One of them was the advocate of the common idolatry; the other the advocate of pantheism. They had been opposing each other on the question of Suttee, the former paper defending the horrid rite with intense fanaticism. They stopped their war, and united their forces against the common enemy, Christianity. There was also a paper in English called *The Enquirer*, the organ of educated natives. The editor, Krishno Mohun Banerji by name, was a Brahman of the highest caste, and of good social position. He was an able man, of liberal sentiments, and, Brahman though he was, dealt terrible blows at the Brahmanical order. There were other educated natives who sympathised and co-operated with him. Their attacks on Hinduism were received with unbounded execration by the rigid Hindus." The editor of *The Enquirer* was disowned by his family. On one occasion an infuriated mob attacked him and his friends, and it was with difficulty they made their escape. He was not a believer in Christianity, but the treatment he received led him to denounce Hinduism still more vehemently. And, as he and his friends had been excommunicated, they resolved upon a crusade against idolatry. At length Krishno Mohun Banerji became a convert to Christianity. He was well known, and his great ability was recognised, in Calcutta. His baptism caused great agitation throughout the city, and became the theme of conversation and discussion with every group that met in street or bazar. From that time he was for many years one of the ablest champions of Christianity in India.

A few years ago, when I took my daily walk in the cool of the evening on the green plain I have described, I sometimes met a venerable man, a noticeable figure. The shadows of life's evening had fallen deeply about him; his bushy eyebrows and beard were white; he had the refined, intellectual features so often seen in Brahmans. But the slow steps, and the downward look, and the hands clasped behind, did not speak so much of extreme age and debility as of peace, meditativeness, a quiet waiting for some coming good. This man was Krishno Mohun Banerji. With him the burning heat of the day was over, and the cool evening had come on. He died in 1885. The following incident is illustrative of the position which Christians and Christianity have taken, since the days of his early struggles, as a recognised power in Indian society. In that great heathen city, Calcutta, a public meeting was held in August, 1885, in the Town Hall, and was attended by men of all classes and different religions. The object of the gathering was to do honour to the memory of a distinguished citizen who had recently died, Krishno Mohun Banerji. It was an occasion of great enthusiasm. Speeches were delivered referring to the great learning, the usefulness, the high character of the deceased Christian citizen. Specially worthy of note is the fact that a Hindu, a Muhammadan, a Brahmo, a Christian, and I think a Parsi, took part in the proceedings. "The path of the just is as the shining light, which shineth more and more unto the perfect day."

The strange unenglish name, *Bhowanipur*, can have but little interest to my readers. What associations it has to me, writing of the place from my English home! Thither I took the young English girl who, more than a third of a century ago, became my wife, and who is still with me. There children were born to us. Thence we carried our dead to the little graves in which they lie beneath an Indian sky. There were smiles for us and tears for us in that Indian home, as is the common lot. We knew laughter and grief, experienced Divine chastenings and Divine comfortings. To Europeans, missionaries as well as others, India is emphatically a land of change. It is a land of happy and not unfruitful work, and also of disappointing and apparently barren toil. Life is saddened by bitter separations: it is consoled by dear friendships. The mind of an old man who has been permitted to remain in one place while many have come and gone, is peopled by the faces and forms of the dead, as well as of the living. All live in the world of his thoughts. So it is with me in regard to the ministers and missionaries of our Calcutta Mission whom I knew during my thirty years of Indian life. They are not a small company. From the venerable Lacroix, the powerful Bengali preacher, the stately, but simple and tender-hearted man who received us into his house when we first landed, down to the young Zenana missionary I welcomed to India just before I left, I saw fifty men and women come and go. In this number I include those I found there, those I left there, and the greater number who both came and went during my Indian life. When a long course of work for the Master, whether as missionary, minister, or in whatever Christian service, has closed, in how tender a light it lies before us as we turn round and look at it! Such as it is, the work lies there unalterable, awaiting the mercy of God, and hoping for the charity of man. When life's solemn evening has come on, little active service remains anywhere. But if, by the fact of advancing years and failing strength, Providence bids us lay down our work and stand aside, we still can serve. For, while the young and strong are rendering active service, "they also serve who only stand and wait." Let it be a comfort to the Lord's servants, that whether standing or speeding at His bidding, doing or suffering,

> "Who best
> Bear His mild yoke, they serve Him best."

CHAPTER III.

IN MY STUDY AND CLASS-ROOM.

ONE Sunday afternoon I was sitting in my study, and with me were three native youths. One of them was a Brahman ; another was of a low caste ; the third was of the warrior caste. It was a gathering of the highest, middle, and lowest. In Hinduism the barriers of caste are insurmountable. To be born a priest, a warrior, a labourer, is to have the whole of fate marked out. The Brahman is a divinity. The Khaist, though inferior, is of the twice-born. But "the self-existent created the Sudra merely for the sake of the Brahman." His whole duty lies in obedience to the higher class.

The three youths had been made one in Christ. They were reading with me a lesson in the evidences of Christianity. In the silent, sultry afternoon, drowsiness came over me, and for a moment or two my thoughts dreamily wandered away into past years. The three young men were no longer before me, but their sires. It came to my mind that twenty years before, the fathers of these three youths were sitting in the same spot with me, engaged, as the sons now were, in studying the Christian evidences. Those earlier students were preparing for evangelistic work. Two of them became preachers of the Word. That Sunday afternoon I received comfort; for I felt that a gracious promise was made good—the sons had taken the place of their fathers. All three of the older generation had entered our mission school as heathen boys. Here were their children receiving my instructions.

Our educational work at Bhowanipur is part of a Christian movement in India which has deeply and widely influenced the peoples of that continent.

What gave rise to so peculiar a mode of missionary work? Why should missionaries take a foreign language to the children of a heathen people, instead of confining themselves to the more obvious way of preaching to adults in their own tongue?

First there is the fact that India is part of our own empire. Where we rule, there we take our language. There is ceaseless intercourse between India and England. When English was introduced into public offices, the natives of India saw that a knowledge of our language would place before them numerous openings to employment in Government and other services. An acquaintance with English was not only the key to knowledge: it opened the door to wealth and distinction. So there sprang up an urgent demand for the education which would enable them to secure these advantages of "posts and pensions." Christian men saw in this intense desire a great opportunity for truth and for Christ. They saw the setting in of a strong flood-tide which might be used to convey to thousands of minds a knowledge of the Gospel. Eager and determined to learn our tongue, they should be led to drink at the fountain of purest English. They should be set to study England's Bible. And they should be introduced to a literature that was impregnated with Christian truth.

An English education, moreover, would call minds back from the dreamland in which they were wandering among strange and monstrous fancies. The wildest absurdities even about natural things formed part of their sacred books. Teach them the simplest truths of geography, and their faith in their Shastras is destroyed. On this point I shall quote the words of a Hindu gentleman writing in the *Calcutta Review* on the "Physical Errors of Hinduism":—

"The Hindu Shastras do not confine their instructions to questions of religion and morality, but everything connected with life and the universe is to be found in their pages. As the religious rites seek to hold sway over all the actions of a man's life, so the sacred writings deal with arts, science, history, etc. All these questions are treated with the same authority, and Brahmans are the authoritative teachers of what is to be found in them. Hence it follows, in innumerable cases, that when men see the physical errors taught with Divine authority in these books, they reject all that is to be found in such bad company.

"The earth rests on the head of the serpent Ananta; the serpent in its turn rests on the back of a tortoise; which in its turn is supported by eight elephants. In the Ramayan, when Rama was about to bend the bow of Siva, his brother, Lukshman, fearing that a great calamity might come from the exertion of such immense force, thus addressed the supporters of the earth: O Earth! do thou support the weight of Rama; O Ananta! do thou sustain the burden of the earth and Rama together; O Kurma Deva! uphold the weight of Rama, the earth, and Ananta, all three combined; and O elephants! do you support the accumulated weight of Rama, Earth, Ananta, and Kurma all put together."

The Vishnu Purana teaches that the world is formed of seven concentric rings, the spans between each belt of land being filled with different liquids: 1. Salt water; 2. Sugar-cane juice; 3. Wine; 4. Ghi; 5. Curds; 6. Milk; 7. Fresh water. These seas were made by one Priyarrata, as he rode round the pre-existent place on his one-wheeled car, and made these seven ruts, which became seven seas. In their measurements of the earth there are great blunders, making it almost large enough to fill up the whole orbit in which it revolves round the sun. And Mount Mera, a mighty mountain, said to be the very centre of the earth, is higher, according to the Puranas, than the distance between us and the moon. And on the lower parts of it again are seven hills, each one fifty-six thousand miles below the other. It will be evident that a Western education must be destructive to faith in the Shastras as a Divine revelation.

They who began this work thought, too, of the influence of early education, the depth and permanence of impressions made in the opening years of life. They experienced how difficult it was to get at the adult mind. It was thickly encrusted with error. The moral sense was, in so many cases, deadened.

The faculty of common sense was weakened. The imagination was filled with impurity. The soul was entangled in the meshes of a vain and subtle system. There were missionaries who said: "Let us go down nearer to the roots of the nation's life. Let us get hold of the young mind, and pre-occupy it with true and pure thoughts before it becomes utterly distorted."

A high authority has said that "Folly is bound up in the heart of a child." Still, to me there is something touching and beautiful in the simplicity, the frankness, the trustfulness which are natural to a child, and in the unsuspecting attitude of a child's mind towards a wise and kind teacher. Its weakness appeals to our pity. Its trustfulness says: "Deal truly with me." I rejoice that children are the same all the world over. May we not say: "Give us the children of a nation, and we will give you a Christian nation"?

In the higher classes the language used, as the medium of education, is English. The range of reading is wide, and there are many opportunities of teaching Divine truth. It has not to be dragged in by violence. It lies on the page to be studied. If Bible lessons are less frequent in these classes of young men than in the lower classes, the opportunities of Christian utterance and influence are not fewer. The missionary is in a class-room with twenty, forty, or even sixty young men before him. He is taking one of the lessons in a course appointed for the University examination. He may be reading the lines of the devout Cowper or the pure and lofty verses of Milton:—

"Come, then, and, added to Thy many crowns,
Receive yet one, the crown of all the earth,
Thou who alone art worthy! Thine it was
By ancient covenant ere Nature's birth,
And Thou hast made it Thine by purchase since,
And overpaid its value with Thy blood."

Or the morning hymn of Adam and Eve:—

"These are Thy glorious works, Parent of good,
Almighty! Thine this universal frame,
Thus wondrous fair: Thyself how wondrous then,
Unspeakable! who sitt'st above these heavens
To us invisible, or dimly seen
In these Thy lowest works; yet these declare
Thy goodness beyond thought and power divine."

A knowledge of the English may be all the students think of or care for. But to give them this, I must show them all that is meant in those English words and sentences. I must rescue Nature from demons, and tell my pupils that it is in the hands of a good Father. I must tell them of One who "hath borne our griefs and carried our sorrows," who "was wounded for our transgressions" and "bruised for our iniquities." If these young men are bent on studying the great masters of the English language, they must ponder the writings of men who bowed in reverence before the Christian religion.

I have often held up the Bible before them in class, and said: "Here is the well-spring of English literature. It is not a specimen, but the fountain." Some of them seemed to think that the Bible could not possibly be equal to Shakespeare or Milton. Sometimes, having explained a fine passage of poetry, and seen that they understood it and felt its beauty, I have said: "Now I'll tell you the original of those lines," and in some glorious psalm I have shown them the idea expressed with more beauty and grandeur. I have heard them say: "Yes, we see; there the Bible surpasses Milton."

The Book of Proverbs I often selected for reading in class. It is the young man's book. It joins itself to the young man on the threshold of life, and sets before him the two divergent ways—the path that leads upwards to gladness and harvest-fields and angels, and the path that leads downwards to bitterness and the black caverns of despair. And all this it does in such a fatherly tone: "My son, hear the instruction of thy father!" An Oriental book, it so often strikes right across the lives, the sins and passions of those Hindu youths. Sometimes, when speaking with the Book of Proverbs before me, I have seen every eye fastened on me, and the silence has been such you might have heard a pin drop. Then have I said within myself: "Now the word is sinking into their hearts. The Lord give it power!" I have heard a young man say of a missionary: "I used to keep away from his Bible class. I could not bear to go. It made me miserable to hear him, and yet remain a Hindu." Many of my pupils listened, and gave no sign of what might be passing in their minds. They finished their course and went away. In some cases I forgot their names and their faces, and lost all recollection of them. But sometimes a letter or a message came, which showed that the seed was living in them. I received a letter, a few years ago, from a young man who had quite passed from my thoughts. A heathen lad he entered the school, a heathen young man for anything I knew he left it. He wrote thus:—

"MY DEAR SIR,—

"I think I need not give you information as to who I am, as I have been a student of your school for more than nine years, and have read with you for more than four years. My poverty has driven me to accept a post here so remote from you all who have poured into my mind the day-spring of the word and the fear of God. But though this has been the case, I know that your warnings, and especially blessings, will always keep me safe from the extreme evil passions of my mind, and from the wiles and fraud of this world. A new life I have found there, and hope God will help me always in the fulfilment of my duties to Him.

"I remember that you once, in your lecture, told us that the blessing of an old and good man comes very near to that of God, for old and good men are His beloved. So I hope, though my presumption may be too bold, you will bless me as you do the other students of your school. I am in heart a student now, and shall remain so for ever. And it is only blessing that I want to have from you.

"I herewith send stamps which I hope will cover the postage of my B.A. certificate, and the Bible I hope to get from you, but by whom [given] I don't know, as a reward of my success in the late B.A. examination.

"That God may always keep you well, and assist you in the furtherance of the work you have taken in hand, is, and shall be, the constant prayer of your most obedient late student."

I have met my "old boys" in many parts of the land, in widely different situations, often grown out of my knowledge. Very respectful they were, very grateful for the instruction they had received. A clerk at some lonely station on the railway, a money-taker at the "zoo," a head-master of a native school, a village doctor, an assistant magistrate, a professor in a college, the "boss" of a company of amateur acrobats, a city shopkeeper, has claimed me as his old teacher. "Sir, don't you know me? I was a pupil of yours." Thus, in out-of-the-way places, on the river, on the plains, among the mountains, I have found a friend in need, or received some mark of kindly feeling. The Lord bless them! May I meet them in the better land!

Soon after my last return to India, I received a letter from an old pupil, apologising for not calling on me to welcome me back, and expressing grateful recollection of the instruction he had received in our institution. He came to see me. I remembered him well—one of our most successful students. His spirit, and manner, and countenance were such as to make me think of the young man who came to Jesus, and "Jesus beholding him, loved him." So I felt towards my old pupil. He was then a medical student.

"Are you a believer in Christ yet?" said I to him. He was not, at least in the way we commonly understand that expression. But he was not a Hindu; he was not an idolater. "I worship the one true God and Father. A few young friends and myself meet together for prayer every week." I have never seen him since. But my thoughts follow such youths. Shall we not meet many of them radiant with joy

JAGADHATRI, WIFE OF MAHADEVA.

in the better life? Surely the good Lord has not lost sight of them.

Mighty changes are taking place in the Indian world of mind. The ancient foundations that have stood unmoved for thousands of years are loosening. Inquiring minds are asking: "What is truth?" Religious spirits are searching after God, and with strong cries beseeching Him to manifest Himself unto them. Some, in a state of unrest, go about from one religious teacher to another asking questions, really desiring light and guidance. We meet them on the road of life, speak with them for a few minutes. They pass on, and we see them no more. A young man one day came into my study, an entire stranger to me. He was exhausted by a long walk in the burning sun. Wiping the perspiration from his forehead, he said:

"Sir, I have come to ask you a few questions."

"Go on," said I.

"Well, sir, my first question is this: How do you reconcile all the misery and evil that are in the world with the goodness and holiness of God?"

"Well," said I, "you have asked a difficult question, one that has perplexed the wisest and best of men in all ages. I cannot profess to be able to solve this great question. I might be able to say something that would mitigate the difficulty a little. But before I attempt that, I should like to ask you a question or two."

I wished to ascertain his notions of the Divine Being, and of human duty and responsibility. He might assume the Pantheist. He might say: "God is the author of sin: man is not responsible: indeed, in a true philosophy sin is not, and goodness is not.'

I said to him : " I suppose you believe, notwithstanding all the misery and evil in the world, that God is good and holy, that sin is contrary to His will and nature ?" He replied, bowing his head reverently : " I have no doubt of it ; God is good and holy." "There's another question," said I ; " we are guilty, and to blame, notwithstanding inclinations within and all inducements to evil outside of us, are we not ?" "Yes," was his reply, " we are guilty, we are to blame. I acknowledge it. I feel it." I was glad to see that he had learnt elsewhere than from Hinduism. " Well then," I said, "we accept that wickedness is, and we believe that God is good and holy." Then I went on to speak as helpfully as I could about the mystery of evil and the sweet uses of adversity.

He remained silent for a time, and then said : " There's another question I want to ask you. Do you believe in auguries and omens ? " Knowing that Hindus are in many cases the slaves of childish and ridiculous superstitions, I said to him : " Tell me more definitely what you mean."

" I mean," said he, " intimations of coming events, things that are sent to give us notice of what is about to happen. The Romans, you know, got omens from noticing the flight of birds. And our sacred books tell us that if any one sneezes in your presence, it's an intimation that some evil threatens you. Our teachers say that this is a proof of the goodness of God ; for we are weak and ignorant creatures, and the sneeze we hear from another is intended to put us on our guard. Now do you believe in such things ? "

I was not disposed to treat the question with

seriousness. "Well," I said, "I'll tell you how I look upon it. When I sneeze, it certainly is a sign to me. It's a sign that I have caught cold. I go out and get very hot, come in and perhaps sit in a draught, and then off I go. So a man sometimes sneezes when he's alone. That is not a sign to somebody else, a kind warning. There's nobody present to get the benefit of it. That would be a wasted sneeze, would it not?"

He smiled and said: "Sir, I no longer believe in these follies and superstitions. I have given them up. I desire to know God, and to get near to Him." He spoke with a deepening earnestness. "Now there is one thing I desire: *I burn for spiritual perfection.*" His earnest words have come back to me a thousand times. In the still morning, before the world is awake and the noises and distractions of the day begin, they have come to my mind. "This should be the tone of my spirit all through this day: I burn for spiritual perfection." "My soul thirsteth for God, the living God." The young man was on his way to a devout countryman of his own, a well-known religious teacher, who resided among the mountains about three hundred miles from Calcutta. "Ah," said he, "he's a good man. His soul is bathed in love. He is filled with peace. When he speaks of God's goodness, his eyes often fill with tears. I think, if I were near him for some weeks, I too should be filled with peace and love." This seeker after God had undertaken a tedious journey of about six hundred miles, hoping to get light and guidance. The teacher he sought was a devout Brahmo—one of the reformed theistic school.

"You know of Jesus Christ?" I asked.

Oh, yes, I have heard and read much of Him."

"Do you not think He was as near to God, as much filled with God, as any human being who ever lived?"

"Yes, I think so."

"Indeed, I may say there was more of God in Jesus than in any religious teacher who has appeared in this world, so far as we know. Don't you think so?"

"Yes."

"Well, then, don't you think it would be well to go to that teacher to learn of God? Why go all the way to the Himalaya Mountains? The Lord is here."

I spoke of Him who is "the brightness of the Father's glory and the express image of His person." So this inquirer, like many others, passed on. I wonder if he remembers the conversation at Bhowanipur as well as I do.

CHAPTER IV.

A CONVERT'S STORY—BY HIMSELF.

I WAS born of Hindu parents. My father brought me up strictly, and taught me all that a Hindu boy should learn about the gods and goddesses. My hair was cut exactly in the orthodox fashion. I grew into a devout Hindu boy, observing all the rites and ceremonies enjoined on boys. I bowed down before every Brahman, and took the dust of his feet and put it reverently on my head, fully believing that such acts were well pleasing to the gods, and at the same time very conducive to my welfare.

When the time came for putting me to an English school, my father sent me to a school entirely under Hindu management. The institution of the London Missionary Society at Bhowanipur was known to be an efficient educational establishment; but my father would not send me there for fear of my becoming a Christian. A youth, an immediate neighbour of ours, had, with other students of the institution, embraced the Christian faith, and my father would not expose me to such a danger. The Hindu school to which I was sent had been got up by the more rigid Hindus as a safe place for their children. There I learned my A B C. As this school could not be compared in regard to efficiency with that conducted by the missionaries, my father was eventually led to send me to the mission institution, simply to secure for me a good English education, and thereby a better prospect of

REV. NUNDO LAL DOSS.

advancement. I was admitted into one of the lowest classes. The books taught here were all different from those taught in the Hindu school. They were full of Scripture stories, both in English and the vernacular. I learned with delight the stories of the Old Testament worthies, and also of the Lord Jesus Christ, just as I had learned of the gods and goddesses by hearing of them or reading some of the popular Hindu books at home. I was very much struck with the miracles of Jesus Christ, and looked upon Him as a very wonderful person, much more wonderful and kind-hearted than Rama or Krishna. I found no difficulty in believing the miracles, as the stories of the Hindu deities abound in miracles, and wonders were said to be still performed by yogees and soothsayers. But I did not believe in Jesus as divine, and still less as the Saviour of men. This truth did not enter my perception at all. I still fully believed in the Hindu gods and goddesses, and dreaded, I cannot say loved, them. I devoutly bowed down before the idols, and silently prayed to them. I had no sense of sin, and therefore never prayed for the pardon of sin, or for moral and spiritual improvement. I only prayed that my life and the lives of my friends, especially that of my father, might be spared; that the gods would not be angry with me; and that I might prosper in life, and have plenty of wealth and learning. The gods, I believed, were always angry, and I prayed to appease their anger.

Three or four years passed in this way, when certain circumstances occurred which increased my devotion to the Hindu gods. A young lad of my own age, a relative, was brought from the country, and placed under my father's care, for the prosecution of his English studies. Fresh from the country, he was full of Hindu superstitions. Reverence for the gods and goddesses was deeply implanted in his mind; and, what was worse, he had no inclination to study. He was looked upon by us boys as a very devout fellow.

He used to say that little attention to study was necessary. Much attention to religious forms and ceremonies would make up for everything. The gods would bless him for his devoutness, and enable him to learn his lessons easily. This was a very agreeable principle of action for a boy of eleven or twelve, as it gave so much more time to play. I need not say I caught the contagion soon, and adopted the very easy course of paying little attention to my studies, leaving it with the gods to make up for the time spent in play. The result of the folly was soon evident. I lost my high place in class; and daily, when my father asked me of my position there, I evaded detection by telling a lie. At last the final test came. The annual examinations were over, and the day came for promotion I was over-devout on the morning of that day. Before starting for school, I stood before a picture of Rama the favourite deity of my relative, and bowed down several times very reverently, and left home fully believing that by virture of my devoutness I should be promoted in school. To my utter disappointment and disgust, my name was not called out for promotion. I became impatient to take my revenge on those who I thought had injured me. No sooner was school dismissed than I went home, and the first thing I did was to take off my shoes, and give the picture of Rama, which I had adored in the morning, a sound thrashing. Fortunately for my relative, my evil genius, he was gone to his native village, or he would have shared the beating with his deity. When the heat of passion was over, fear arose in my mind. It was not the fear that the god would be angry with me. It was the fear of my father's anger. The picture was placed near the doorway leading into the room where he performed his morning and evening devotions, and he bowed down before it when he started to his office and when he returned home. The marks of my shoe-nails were left on the paper. He was sure to see them, and he would not let the offender go unpunished. The punishment would certainly be heavy, as shoe-beating was the worst indignity that could be offered, especially to a god. And what was worse, the offender was his own son. In addition to all this, I was not promoted at school. I took a piece of chalk and tried to hide the nail marks. I partially succeeded, and was glad to find that they escaped my father's notice. Afterwards I began to pay more attention to my studies, and no longer sought the kind offices of the gods by bribing them with a little extra devotion. But my faith in them as objects of worship still remained, though little by little it decreased, as I made progress in my studies.

In April, 1851, six students of the senior class openly professed their faith in Christ and renounced Hinduism. Three of them subsequently entered the ministry, and are still serving as ordained missionaries in North India. The baptism of these six youths threw the Hindu society of Bhowanipur into convulsions. Through fright many withdrew their children from the mission school. My father was one of the first to do so. I was sent back to the Hindu school, where I continued for three years. No religious knowledge whatever was imparted there, and the subject of religion never troubled my mind. But my antipathy to Christians and Christianity became more developed; why, I cannot say. Faith in the gods imperceptibly died away; still I outwardly conformed to Hindu rites and ceremonies, and bowed down before idols and Brahmans.

At last my father, anxious for my education, was induced to send me back to the mission school. Here I found myself in a different element. Religion was not only taught in the class, it was also talked of by the students out of class. By coming in contact with class-fellows who were Brahmos, I became a theist, believing in one true God, the author of the universe, who alone is to be worshipped. One day a man brought a stone image of Shitola, the goddess of small-pox, to my father's house, and asked for presents for her. The presents were, of course, for himself. Many men make their living by the name of some god whose image they profess to keep and worship for the benefit of the community. Shitola is held in great dread. The man began to sing out her dreadful attributes, and how she takes vengeance on those who despise her. With my new faith in one only true God, and my sense of the foolishness of idol-worship, I could not put up with these vain threats of revenge and boasts of power. I asked him to give me some of the flowers with which the little figure was worshipped. Thinking I wanted them to ingratiate myself with the goddess, he readily gave me a few. I instantly threw them on the ground and trampled on them. "Tell your goddess," I said, "to do me any harm she can for thus insulting her. She cannot do me harm, for there is no such being." The man was horrified. He flew into a rage, cursed me, and left the house. This was the first time I openly broke away from idolatry, or unnecessarily wounded the feelings of any man by wantonly affronting the object of his worship. Still I was not without misgivings. I had not been inoculated or vaccinated, and the thought troubled me that in case there really were such a goddess, the most dreadful consequences might follow my affronting her. But these fears soon passed away.

My zeal in the cause of theism increased every day, and I began to attend Brahmo worship. With my zeal for theism, my antipathy towards Christianity also increased. The influence of one of my class-fellows had to do with this. His brother had published a work of Tom Paine's, and the younger brother tried to infuse an anti-Christian spirit into our minds at class. A missionary had issued an edition of Watson's Apology as an antidote to Tom Paine, but we never troubled our heads with reading that. We took Tom Paine for an oracle, and imbibed his spirit. During the Scripture lessons we tried to bring forward as many infidel arguments as we could; and instead of trying to learn what was taught in the Scriptures, we only raised objections.

It happened that one of our class-fellows was an earnest inquirer into the truth of Christianity. Besides reading in class, he used to visit the missionary in his house. Somehow or other this fact oozed out. Then all our anti-Christian zeal was exerted to keep this young man from becoming a Christian or inquiring into Christianity. Our spare moments were employed in plying him with infidel arguments and taunts. We gave him no peace. He tried to the best of his ability to answer us. One day, as we were going home from college, five or six of us were troubling him on the road. He became quite agitated, and, standing still, he addressed us most solemnly in the following words :—

"You may say anything you like against Christianity. Whether I am able to answer your objections or not does not matter. Christianity will not be a loser or gainer by that. There is one thing which I cannot get over. I should like to know whether you can?"

I asked him what it was, and he said :—

"I am a sinner, and everybody admits that he is a sinner. I feel I cannot save myself. I need a Saviour. What do you say to that?"

These last words went as an arrow to my heart. I felt I too was a sinner. Certainly I could not save myself. I was struck dumb. I never spoke a word to him after to find fault with him. My peace of mind was gone. Hitherto I had looked upon myself as a very wise young man, much wiser than the Hindu idol-worshipper. I was also much wiser than the Christian who worships a man—Jesus. But all my wisdom melted away into nothingness. I then thought that perhaps the Christ of the Bible could save me; and yet I felt averse to accept Him. However, I made up my mind to read the Bible and the "Evidences" with attention. But I kept all these thoughts to myself. I knew what would follow if my class-fellows or others came to know my state of mind. Little by little the light dawned on my mind, and, by God's great grace, I found Christ was the Saviour I needed.

With this new faith new difficulties arose. When I entered the mission college I said to myself: "If I am ever convinced of the truth of Christianity, I will never openly be a Christian." I determined now to keep to that resolution. To confess Christ meant to be separated from everybody and everything one holds dear on earth. I said to myself: "God knows my heart, and also knows my difficulties. He will mercifully excuse me for remaining a secret Christian." I continued in this state for about two years, during which I regularly read my Bible and prayed. For this purpose I used to resort to the roof of my father's house, where there was little disturbance from others, and where none would find out how I was engaged.

These two years of secret Christian life were not without their trials. My faith was put to the test on two occasions. Once I was taken ill with something like cholera. I took medicine; but, as a panacea for all evils, devout Hindus have recourse to something sacred. When they return from a pilgrimage to the temple of Juggernath at Pooree, they bring back some of the boiled rice that is presented to the idol. It dries up and becomes hard in a few hours. Devout people keep a stock of this sacred rice in their homes, and swallow a grain of it every day. I used to see my father take a grain after his morning bath and devotions. He put it very reverently down his throat, and then rubbed his head with the fingers with which he had taken it out, as if the blessing of Juggernath would rest there for this act of devotion. It is also administered to people in illness, as a charm to drive away disease. When I was ill some one suggested to my father that it should be administered to me, and he took out a grain from the sacred pot and brought it to me. I said to myself: "If I die of this disease,—and ten chances to one I shall die of it,—it must not be with a lie on my lips. I trust in Christ for salvation, and I must not take this rice as if I had faith in that false god." So I refused to take it, and on my father asking the reason, I told him I did not believe in its efficacy. He was dreadfully annoyed, and looked fiercely at me, and if I had not been ill he would have beaten me.

The next trial was much severer. I was reading my New Testament one evening in an outer room of the house, when a Brahman neighbour, a man of a very angry temperament, came in to see my father, and took his seat near me. He could make out at once that I was reading the New Testament, but he asked:—

"What book is that?"

"The New Testament," I said.

"Do not read that book," said he; "what it teaches is all false."

"Have you ever read the book?" I asked.

"No," he replied.

"Is it proper for you to call the book false without reading it?"

This incensed him, and he called out:—

"The Bible is false, and Jesus Christ is false. Kali is a real goddess, and, if she chose, she could kill you this moment, on the spot."

This was too much for me. In the fervour of my faith in Christ I made use of some expressions most derogatory to the honour of Kali, and then I challenged her to kill me that night. The rage of the Brahman knew no bounds. He was almost mad with fury, and cursed both me and my father aloud. My father was inside, engaged in his evening devotions. He heard the noise, and inquired what it was about. The Brahman told him the story, angrily and with imprecations, and appealed to him to deal out justice to such a wretch of a son, and stop him from bringing disgrace on the family. My father then came out hurriedly, and asked :—

"Have you really used such language against Kali?"

"Yes," said I.

"Why have you done so?"

"Because I believe that Kali is no more a goddess than any piece of stone on the road."

"Oh," said he, "my goddess Kali is false! Is your Jesus Christ true?"

"Yes," I replied.

He said nothing more, but came up and taking hold of the hair of my head, slipped off his wooden sandal and belaboured me until I fell to the ground, stunned. On recovering I found that our next-door neighbour, a Brahman, who was very fond of me, had come to my rescue, and was covering me to shield me from further violence. The elderly female members of the house had also come out to see what had happened, and they all besought my father not to strike me any more. He then came up to me, and taking hold of me by the neck, pushed me into the streets, in the dark, saying: "Leave my house! I will see how your Christ feeds you." My deliverer, the Brahman, came to me and consoled me. He said: "Your father's anger will soon be appeased, and for the present I will take you in, but you must not speak against the gods." Though my faith in Christ was as strong as ever, I was not prepared to forsake father and home to follow Him. A few minutes after I was taken back to the house. My father was much pacified. He said : "Well, you have come back. Remain at home now, and do not stir from the house. Do not go to school again." From that night I was kept a close prisoner. Three weeks passed in this way, and I showed no inclination to go out. This perhaps led my father to think that his beating had driven my faith in Christ out of me. But in this he was mistaken. I was more confirmed in my faith, and felt joy in being able to suffer for Christ.

During this time I increased in my knowledge of Christian truth. There were other secret disciples like myself. I found from conversation with my cousin, and a neighbour, both of them my class-fellows, that they too were believers. A very large number, if not the majority, of students in the upper classes of missionary institutions, believe in Christ, though only a few accept Him openly. The young man whose words first attracted me to Christ, never made open profession of his belief. I met him several times after my baptism, and asked him why he did not confess his faith. He said he fully believed in Christ, but he could not come forward as a professed believer, for that would break the heart of his widowed mother and his aunt, to whom he was all in all, and who were staunch Hindus. It is now years since I saw him, and I am told he is dead The Lord is his judge. There are many like him in the Hindu community.

One Sunday evening in December, 1856, a woman brought news of several deaths which had occurred in the house of a cousin who lived fourteen miles from Calcutta. We all came out of our rooms to hear the sad story, which she delivered standing in the open quadrangle of the Zenana. Seven persons, she said, had died in the house in a fortnight, all of cholera. She related that returning one day from the cremation of one of the family, they found that another had expired during their absence. A fear struck me: "If I were to die as suddenly, what would become of my soul? Here I am, a believer in Christ, but acting like a hypocrite. I have never confessed Christ." I was overtaken with a great terror. Trembling I sat down, and resolved I would no longer delay, but would declare my faith as soon as the approaching college examinations were over. My anxiety increased as the time drew near for breaking away for ever from my home and Hindu society.

On the day fixed for leaving home, I wrote a letter to my father, in which I stated my intention of becoming a Christian, and that I left home for that purpose. In the evening he, with several friends, came to see me, and tried to dissuade me from my purpose. For the next three days there was no rest for me. My friends and relatives plied me with arguments. At times they taunted me, but oftener they tried to work on my affections. They told me that I could live like a Christian, and would be allowed to do so at home, provided I was not baptised. They brought persons well up in infidel arguments to speak with me. When all their resources failed, my father began to shed tears, and cried like a little child. This was the most dreadful of all the trials I had to pass through. Even now it sends a pang through my heart as I think of it after more than thirty-four years. He passed his arms under mine, and pressed me to his breast, and weeping said: "Come home with me, and do not be a Christian. It breaks my heart to think of it. You will be the cause of my death. Come home with me, or I shall die." Oh! that was a most fearful trial, but grace was given me to endure it. Seeing his last attempt fail, he changed. His anger was awful. "I see," he said, giving vent to his indignation, "you will not change your mind. Go, then, and be a Christian or whatever you like. But never see my face again. Do not dream of entering my house. If you come there, I will kill you, or kill myself. You are no more my son. You are dead to me." So saying, he turned his back on me, and kept his word for full seven years. During those years he would not see me, nor receive any message from me. Once I saw him accidentally on the street. As soon as he caught sight of me he turned his face and went in another direction. The house was forbidden me, but I went in his absence to see my female relatives. My mother had died when I was only three years old. After seven years he spoke to me, and permitted me to visit the house. Afterwards he became very friendly, and even invited me now and then to partake of food. But neither he nor any other member of the house sat with me when I ate. I had my share given me on a plantain leaf. Later on a plate was kept for my use only, and when eating I had to sit in a corner by myself. He was a strict Hindu, and caste rules were most rigidly observed in our house. Subsequently he consulted me on all family matters, but never for a single night was I allowed to sleep under his roof. He never suffered me to approach him on the subject of religion, but he admitted that it was purely from religious motives that I became a Christian, for he could not believe, he said, that anything but religion could draw me away from him whom I loved so much. He died in June, 1890, in the sacred city of Benares, whither he had gone as a rigid Hindu to end his days. I was baptised on the 11th of January, 1857.

The writer of the above story is the Rev. Nundo Lal Doss, who, by the invitation of the directors of the London Missionary Society, visited England in 1887, and addressed many audiences in this country and the Australian colonies with great acceptance.

CHAPTER V.

THE OLD BRAHMAN.—"GIVE ME MY WIFE AND CHILDREN."

AMONG the regular contributions I received for our work in Bengal, one was from a man who lived about seven hundred miles from us in the country of Oudh. He was quite a stranger to me. His name, Kali Choron Banerji, showed him to be a Brahman. With the donation he usually wrote a word or two: "I send this for the preaching of the Gospel," or "You know for what purpose." I became desirous to know something of this stranger, and to have an explanation of his interest in our mission. I asked some of our oldest Christians if they knew the man. By degrees a touching human history opened up to me, of a kind which has not been uncommon in our work among high-caste Hindus, a history of suffering and wrong, the wrenching of the closest ties of nature, faithfulness to God and truth. The story will illustrate the trials of some of our early converts.

Kali Choron Banerji was almost the first convert through our work in the Missionary College. Nearly half a century ago, he professed Christ by baptism. When my thoughts were first drawn to him, the missionaries who had taught and baptised him, and friends who had sympathised with him in his early trials, were long since dead. At his baptism at Union Chapel in 1843, Mr. Boaz told the story of his conversion. Micaiah Hill, of Berhampur, commended him to God in prayer. He then delivered up his Brahmanical thread, and was received into the fellowship of the Church. He was twenty-two years of age, a man of property, and a member of one of the most respectable families in Bhowanipur, where he had lived in the family house with his elder brother. By his mother's side he was joint proprietor of the neighbouring temple of Kali. Immediately after his baptism, Kali Choron went to live in the house of a Christian friend, since no return to his Hindu home was possible. But he longed for his wife and two little children—the youngest a babe he had never yet seen—who were at the house of his father-in-law at Nuddea, many miles from Calcutta. One day he started for Nuddea to bring them away. The father-in-law and brothers-in-law refused to let him see them, or even enter the house, and drove him from the door. They threatened to beat him if he remained near it. The poor young fellow in his trouble addressed a petition to the magistrate of the place, praying for an order to the father-in-law to produce the wife and children in court for the purpose of delivering them to him, their husband and father. The order was issued, but it seems to have been easily and safely evaded. Immediately it was served, the father-in-law despatched the woman and her children to Calcutta, to the house of Kali Choron's brother at Bhowanipur. Instead of appearing in court he sent his son, who coolly informed the magistrate that the petitioner's wife and children had gone to Calcutta. The magistrate contented himself with telling the husband that the case was not in his jurisdiction, and so dismissed it. Nothing was said of the evasion of the magistrate's order and the contempt of court. Our young Christian returned to Calcutta, and wrote to his brother asking for his wife and children. He received no reply. He went to the house, and was treated as he had been at Nuddea with abuse and rejection.

These two brothers, with their widowed mother and two sisters, had lived together for years in the dwelling-house of their late father. The elder son was now head of the family; here, then, the young wife and her two little ones were in the possession and under the rule of the elder brother. How was the man to get his own? Taking two Christian friends with him, he resolved to go to the house and bring them away. He was refused access to them, and turned out of the house.

But the battle must not be given up. He would try what redress he could get from an English magistrate in the British capital. He had been told, by an old female servant of the family, that his wife was willing to come to him if she could get away. In a petition to the magistrate, he declared his belief that his wife was detained against her own will by his brother, who also refused to let him see her and his children. He humbly begged that the brother should be ordered to produce them before the magistrate for the purpose of their being delivered up to him, unless the wife, in such presence, should positively refuse to accompany him and live with him.

The magistrate did not issue the order. He sent a deputy to the house to inquire of the wife whether she was willing to go to her husband. Kali Choron himself was present at the inquiry. Let the reader imagine the scene. The "interview" is held with a curtain between the parties specially and vitally concerned. On one side of the purda is the officer with the husband, and probably other males; within the purda is the wife surrounded by relatives, who have tutored and terrified her into compliance with their wishes. She had not seen her husband for many months, and had been made to believe he had undergone some horrible transformation by the dreadful step he had taken. The officer makes the inquiry. She is heard to say, "she does not wish to go with her husband; she wishes to stay where she is." But her tears and agitation and broken voice show that her heart does not go with her words. Her words, however, are declared by the official to settle the matter. The husband received his dismissal. If only the man and woman had been left together, as right was they should be, the wife with the husband she had loved and still loved, the father of her children, the man she had taken "for better or for worse," to live with him till death should part them, how different would have been the result! He would have shown why he had become a Christian. He would have assured her of his undiminished affection, and she would have believed him. He would have told her he needed the comfort of her companionship, and that it was his desire and his duty as a Christian to cherish and honour her more than he had done when he was a heathen. Who can doubt what the result would have been?

"Love is lord of all," sings the old poet. Nature is beautiful, strong, right. The redress which the young man had sought in vain from court and magistrate was brought about in the good providence of God. A native newspaper charged the young Christian with folly in supposing his wife would join him. Missionaries had declared their belief that if she were allowed to act according to her own feelings she would go to him. They judged from the principles of human nature, principles implanted by the hand of God; and they knew the circumstances of this particular case. But they were declared by native writers to be utterly ignorant of the native character. They would be taught now, it was said, how much a Hindu woman would sacrifice for her religion.

Kali Choron believed what the old servant had quietly told him of his wife's willingness to join him, if she could escape from her bondage. He understood the tearful and trembling refusal at the sham interview. By the help of the old servant there was a real interview, or some secret arrangement was made. Flight was agreed upon. The wife watched. The opportunity came. With her little boy she stole away from the house to her beloved. How I should like to ask the old Brahman the particulars of this event of fifty years ago—the flight of the secluded, timid Hindu girl! Was it by night or by day? Had the old servant at the family home helped them, dear hearts, to come together? Had a trysting-place been appointed where he waited for his wife and child? Here is a story for a novelist. I know so well the roads along which they would hurry in their flight, the gate by which they would enter the mission settlement.

When it was found that the mother had gone, it occurred to the elder brother that it was of no use to keep the baby! so the baby was sent to her. And then, considering the circumstances, he kindly consented that his younger brother should have his wife and children, seeing they were already with him! But now came the question of his share of the paternal property. In many cases our young converts have had to renounce wealth, as well as the society and affection of relatives and friends, for the sake of the Gospel. This, the old report says, was the first recorded instance of a convert recovering, not only wife and children, but his paternal property also. Still he consented to an arrangement highly advantageous to those who had cast him off, and who, whatever sacrifices he might make in their favour, would ever treat him as an outcast. He returned kindness for cruelty.

When I first knew of him he was an old man. He held a Government clerkship yielding only a small salary. To the end of my stay in India I received his regular and liberal contribution for the preaching of the Gospel among his countrymen. "O Lord, ... the Gentiles shall come unto Thee from the ends of the earth, and shall say, Surely our fathers have inherited lies, vanity, and things wherein there is no profit."

CHAPTER VI.

BEFORE THE MAGISTRATE.—A MONSTER MEETING.

THE court and the adjoining quadrangle were crowded with people intensely interested in the trial. A missionary was charged with the abduction of two young Brahmans, for the purpose of baptising them. In the first case, the prosecutor was the father of the convert. When the trial had been duly opened, the magistrate said: "It will simplify and expedite matters to hear the statement of the young man himself." Accordingly he related the history of his convictions, gave his reason for wishing to profess himself a Christian, and, in the strongest terms, declared he had not been forced in any way. The missionary then gave his answer to the charge—a simple, lucid, convincing relation of facts. When he concluded, the father said: "I wish to carry the case no further. I had been given to understand that my son was kept in close confinement by the Padri Sahib, and was weeping to return to his home. Therefore, I brought the present suit. As I now hear from himself that this is not the case, I give up the suit, son, and all."

It was curious that in the second case the prosecutor was a little boy of about ten years old, the convert's cousin and co-heir. The father-in-law brought forward the question of the youth's age, and declared him to be a minor. In witness, he placed his horoscope, or birth-register, before the magistrate. Every respectable Hindu family keeps a record of the birth of a child. The astrologer of the family prepares a paper, and therein notes the day, hour, and minute of the child's birth. The position of the heavenly bodies at the time is also recorded; and if a child is born under unlucky stars, the greatest care is taken by the observance of religious ceremonies to propitiate the god of Fate, and avert threatened danger. These papers are consulted before a marriage, to ascertain and compare the "stellar mansions" under which the boy and girl were born. If the signs are found antagonistic, negotiations for marriage are sometimes broken off. The horoscope is of real value in courts of justice, for verifying the exact age of a person. In the present trial it showed that the convert's age was only fifteen years and nine months. This seemed decisive against the missionary. But the moment the youth saw the paper, he called out to the magistrate: "This is not mine, sir; I know my own well, and it is much smaller than this." Its clean and fresh appearance produced the same conviction on the gentleman appealed to. "Certainly," he said, "it is wonderful paper to have lasted so long, and yet look so clean." Obviously it was a forged document. The father-in-law could only say: "Sir, what does he know about religion; and how can he be allowed to act for himself?" The magistrate replied : " You allow lads of his age and even younger to apply for situations in public offices ; they become writers in the Treasury and other places ; they get salaries ; they marry. And is it only on the subject of religion they must have no opinion of their own ? " He concluded the case by telling the two young men they were at liberty to go where they liked, and they left the court with the missionaries and other friends. To be dragged into courts of law was distressing to the missionaries ; but the result of the trial was favourable to the prosecution of their work among the young. An important point had been settled in public court ; namely, that a youth of seventeen was allowed to think for himself in the matter of religion. The decision was awaited with deep interest among the native community. Before three hours had passed it was known for miles around that the missionaries had won the day.

At that time, in the course of three months, six of our students made a public profession of their faith in Christ, and were baptised before large and deeply interested congregations in Union Chapel. It was evident that many others shared in their convictions, though the appalling difficulties in the way of a profession hindered them from the like public testimony. In the class-room the missionary sometimes witnessed a vehement repudiation of idolatry.

The festival in honour of the goddess Durga—" the Durga pujah "—is a universal holiday in Bengal. Thousands of men, almost all of them clerks, whose work is in the city, away from their families, go then to their village homes. Government offices, houses of business, schools and colleges, are all closed for

UNION CHAPEL, CALCUTTA.

about twelve days. It is a season of happy family gatherings, as Christmas is with us, and as such may continue to hold its place when Hinduism has passed away. But it is also, with multitudes, especially in the city, a time of licentious indulgence and mad idolatry. We always feared the injurious influence of this holiday upon our students. Just before the pujah, a missionary was exhorting his class to resist the temptations they would meet to impurity and idolatry. "Sir," they said, "we would rather die than worship Durga. All we want is to see our friends."

When a Brahman boy is invested with the sacred thread—poita—at the age, it may be, of nine, he assumes all the authority and privileges of Brahmanhood. The poita must be worn ever after, and never for a moment cease to be in contact with the body. I have seen a student take it off in class and throw it on the desk, with the words: "See, sir! Do you think we care about these things?"

Such inroads on the dominions of Hinduism caused consternation in the native community, and called forth determined opposition. The school was nearly broken up. Some of the leaders of Hindu society seemed resolved to make every effort to check the progress of Christianity. It was resolved to call a "monster meeting." An immense gathering was expected. The residents of the city and suburbs were invited. A day of leisure with natives—Sunday—was chosen. The meeting was not a success. Only about five hundred were present of the great population supposed to be specially interested. Not many influential and wealthy natives attended, and the more liberal portion of the community appear to have held back. The news of these movements found its way into *The Times*, and was the subject of remark in many English newspapers.

Two things especially were noticeable in the meeting. First, the native gentleman who presided spoke in defence of the missionaries; and, secondly, a large majority of those assembled acknowledged they could not check the progress of English education. One speaker said that though English was not necessary to salvation, it was, at least, the road to wealth. This argument seems to have carried the meeting. The following important question was discussed, whether any one who had violated caste by becoming a Christian, or by eating with Christians, could, by penance and absolution, be received back into Hindu society. The president thought this desirable, and set forth a process by which it might be effected. He read a mode of restoration, but seemed to think it impracticable, as the constitution of many might break down under the severity of the ordeal. It was therefore to be commuted to a fine of kine and cowries, the value to be regulated according to the caste of the offender. It was thought necessary, however, to take the opinion of the teachers of the law, the pundits, who were present. They were not helpful. "Can the offender be restored to the privileges of social life?" was the inquiry put to them. Their reply was cautious. They could answer for the religious but not for the social side of the question. A man so offending might certainly have his sins forgiven, but they could not answer for his restoration to social life. A few sensible men in the meeting urged the importance of establishing schools of their own that should cope with missionary institutions. This practical suggestion, however, was overborne by the great question of restoration for lapsed Hindus.

And yet in this suggestion lay the solution of their difficulty. It was disregarded at the time. They have realised its importance since. In recent years schools and colleges established by natives and under native management have had a marked success They have been successful in the direction most valued by Hindus; that is, in preparing their students to pass University examinations. They have rivalled, and in some instances surpassed, colleges established by Government, and provided with accomplished and highly paid professors from the English Universities. Hence they have attracted crowds of students.

Some think that this native movement threatens the very existence of mission schools. The flood-tide of popularity which filled our colleges seems to be receding, and the ebb may possibly leave our educational institutions high and dry, emptied of pupils. But the success of the Gospel is not endangered thereby. We need not be alarmed. God fulfils Himself in many ways. Providence led us into this educational work. Providence may lead us out of it into other paths. It has proved mighty in the breaking down of that system which, on this earth, is emphatically the stronghold of idolatry. It is the only form of work which has influenced the higher castes. It has supplied us with a large number of educated and able preachers of the Word. Its fruit in the cities is an intelligent and influential, though comparatively small Christian community. It has swelled by scores of thousands the numbers who can be addressed in English. Any preacher from England, though he does not understand a word of the vernacular, can, from the first day of his arrival in Calcutta, find large audiences who can perfectly understand all he says.

Missionary societies have been repeatedly urged to withdraw from the work of education in India. Some years ago the committee of one of the societies, in order to obtain an expression of opinion as to the desirability of maintaining their colleges, sent circulars of inquiry to a number of gentlemen of Indian experience, but not missionaries. I shall quote two or three sentences from the reply of Sir W. W. Hunter. "I should regard any withdrawal of . . missions from the work of education as disastrous. The weak point in our system of public instruction is our inability to give any form of religious teaching in our State schools. We cannot teach Christianity, for the greater proportion of the taxpayers are Hindus and Muhammadans. We cannot teach Hinduism or Islamism, for we are a Christian government. The result is an absence of religious teaching of any sort, which the natives of India deeply deplore."

Wide-spread excitement, deep and painful agitation marked the early days of the educational work. The houses of missionaries were besieged by threatening crowds; converts, in interviews with grieved and exasperated relatives and others, were tried almost beyond endurance. Some were quite overcome; some were carried off by violence. Missionaries had to defend themselves in courts of justice. In the crowded court at Alipore, the defendant was accompanied by brethren of the same mission, Messrs. Boaz,

Mullens, Paterson, and Parker. I am writing of events forty years after they occurred. Of all the brethren so deeply concerned in these early struggles, the accused missionary, Mr. Storrow, is the sole survivor. Of the rest, the one who was longest among living men was laid in an African grave many years ago. So the tide of the years rises higher and higher about us; and, one after another, our co-workers and companions disappear from our sight. But "the word of the Lord liveth and abideth for ever." A poet has written,—

> "When musing on companions gone,
> We doubly feel ourselves alone."

But with the feeling of loneliness there is also joyous expectation. There is the upward look of faith and hope,—

> "They're all gone to that world of light,
> And I alone am lingering here."

CHAPTER VII.

SHEPHERDS OF THE EAST FOR EASTERN FLOCKS.

IT was Henry Martyn, I think, who said that if he could see a Brahman truly converted to God, he should consider it the greatest miracle the world ever witnessed. At this day how many of the priestly caste are truly Christian men and—preachers of the Word! The idea is common in this country that Brahmans are the most difficult class to move. My own experience among the young does not coincide with that opinion. A large proportion of the converts from our educational work have been of the priestly class. Indeed, the majority of those who, within my knowledge, have become Christian teachers of the people have been of this caste. The Banerjis, Mookerjis, Chaterjis, Haldars, are all Brahmans. How often do these names appear in missionary reports from North India!

Tara Prasad Chaterji is the oldest of the native preachers of our Calcutta Mission. Forty years ago five youths, all Brahmans, came from their Hindu homes resolved to embrace the Christian faith. Three of them yielded to the pressure brought to bear on them by friends, and went back. Of the two who remained firm, Tara Prasad Chaterji was one. He has been a zealous missionary and a faithful shepherd of Christ's flock for many years. I give his story very nearly in his own words. Some readers will recognise in it features peculiar to Indian life. There is the respectable family-house in an obscure village. India is a land of villages rather than cities; and the traveller in remote places comes upon solitary mansions in wide, quiet districts of rice-fields, and amid hamlets of miserable huts. There is the indigenous village school, held by permission in some verandah of the big house, or out in the open, with sky as roof, where a dozen or two of little boys, mostly naked, sing the multiplication table, learn to cast simple accounts for village shop-keeping, and to read and write Bengali. There is the necessary removal to the great town or to some station where there is an English school. There is the fear in the well-ordered, strict Hindu home lest the simple village lad should be ruined by the vices of the town. There is the heavy blow that suddenly falls upon the house when it is found that the beloved lad, the only son too, has done something more dreadful, more hopeless than indulging in vice—he has become a Christian. A profligate son might remain in his Hindu home an accepted member of society and adherent of the Hindu religion. He can perform, as no one else can, those last ceremonies necessary to the repose of his father's soul. But the son who embraces Christianity is as if he had never been—except to bring disappointment, bitterness, and despair. Then there is the touching interview between the dying Hindu father and his Christian son.

"I was born," writes Tara Babu, "at a village about nine miles south-east of Calcutta. My family was that of a Kulin Brahman and was well-to-do.

"Up to the age of nine I stayed in my native village, and went to the village school, which was held in our family-house. At the age of ten I was taken to Calcutta for the sake of learning the English language, and lived for a few months at our second family-house at Bhowanipur. When I was eleven I was removed to Chinsurah, the old Dutch settlement on the river Hoogley, about sixteen miles above Calcutta. I joined my two youngest uncles, who were carrying on their studies in the college there. The object was to keep me from city evils and bad companions. There I began the English language. The principal of the college was Captain Richardson. He was kind-hearted and exceedingly fond of the boys, with whom he used to play after school hours. He pleased them, too, by gifts of sweetmeats. By these means he gathered a large number of boys around him. Every day also out of school hours he collected advanced students in his drawing-room, to give them lessons from his own book, 'Richardson's Selections.' He showed them pictures and talked on different subjects. So he was loved by all. The boys of the school looked up to the Captain as their personal friend.

"One Saturday afternoon, when I was about fifteen, I heard and noticed, for the first time, the name of the Lord Jesus. Our principal was reading to us from his 'Selections.' One of the senior boys asked him who Christ was, and what His work was upon the earth. In reply he impressively related the life, and explained the mission, of Christ. I was much impressed with his words. This led me to ask him how I could get to know more about Christ. He sent me with a letter to the military chaplain of the station. I went to him from time to time, but my going was of no effect, as he could not find time to speak to me. He kindly gave me, however, a copy of the New Testament, which I prized much. One evening, when I was reading it, my youngest uncle asked me what book I was reading. Finding it was the New Testament, he snatched it from me, and set fire to it.

"That year, owing to family misfortunes, we left Chinsurah, and removed to our family-house at Bhowanipur. With this sudden change of circumstances, my desire to know more about Christ grew cool and died away. Also, I confess it with shame, though I was young in years, by mixing with evil companions, I became too free in my habits,—in fact, I led a sinful life, and forgot all about my spiritual welfare. At this time I was reading in the Government Hindu College in Calcutta. This added fuel to the fire of evil passion. Almost every evening, after coming from the college, I and my companions used to visit the Bhowanipur Bazaar Chapel, with the deliberate intention of disturbing the Christian preachers. Often we pelted Mr. Lacroix, Dr. Mullens, and the Bengali preachers with stones.

"In January, 1850, I had a severe attack of fever and dysentery. This illness led me to think seriously about my sins and salvation. Then the course of my life changed. I regularly attended the preaching places, heard the word with attention, and began to love the men I had hated.

"One day I resolved I would open my mind to any preachers who might be at the chapel that evening. It happened that Dr. Mullens was there. When he was on his way home, I went up to him and asked whether I could be favoured with a copy of the New Testament. 'Yes, my boy,' he answered, 'you can have one this evening if you will come to my house.' I went with him to his study. He asked me to sit, and talked with me in such a way as to show me that he was concerned for my welfare. Then he gave me a copy of the New Testament, and prayed with me. He advised me to come to his school, as by so doing I should get many opportunities of seeing the missionaries and reading the Bible. These were the things he impressed on me that evening: that I was a sinner, that I needed a Saviour, that Christ was the only Saviour for me, that the time of salvation was the present.

"After this I had to suffer persecution for attending the Bhowanipur mission school. Daily instruction in Christianity thoroughly convinced me of my sinfulness, and confirmed my faith in Jesus. At the end of a few months my mind was made up to embrace the faith. This resolution I expressed to my class teacher, who with joy told me that there were others wishing to become Christians. When I inquired who they were, he mentioned the names of four young men. We commenced then to talk to each other, and visited our teacher's house every day. Saturday, the 12th of April, was fixed upon for coming out openly and finally. Accordingly, at the appointed time, we five came to the school, and thence went to the house of Mr. Storrow.

"Before closing, Dr. Mullens announced to the whole school what we had done. Rapidly the dreadful news reached our respective homes. Soon, relatives and friends, with a number of low-class ruffians, came to attack the house. An immense crowd quickly gathered. Europeans from the neighbourhood and the police came to our help. Two of the inquirers were induced by their friends to go away. Each of them assured us he would return on the morrow for baptism. Another had yielded earlier. The time was critical for us who remained. Fear, sorrow, and affection all came upon us, and extreme heaviness. In the minds of the missionaries, too, there was much anxiety. Some of them even spoke of our being sent back to our homes. The Almighty gave us strength according to our need. The next day, Sunday, April 13th, 1851, we were baptised. So far our fears were over. We felt settled and comforted. On Monday our relatives lodged complaints with the magistrates, and on Wednesday we and the European missionaries and others appeared in court. The magistrate dismissed the case. We lived for about two months in the house of a missionary in the city, because of repeated attempts to take us away.

"Now a word or two about my dear father. After the trial, in the presence of the magistrate, he said: 'Here, in the name of my God, I declare that from this moment my son is dead to me. As long as I live, I will never see his face; he is dead to me and my family.' This vow he kept for full twenty years.

During this time he would not see me, and also forbade others to mention my name in his hearing. It was through the kindly intervention of an English gentleman he at length gave way. After twenty long years I again saw my dear father's face. The first interview was heartrending. For an hour father and son looked at each other speechless and sobbing, and then separated. Not until twelve years after this first interview was he perfectly reconciled to me. Afterwards I paid frequent visits to him. Every time I went he was generous ; he gave me money, he often gave me good counsel, and asked me when I would go again.

"Four days before his death, he was eager to see me. A message was sent to the village manse at Karapukur, where I was living among the people whose pastor I was. My father had gone to Tribany, a holy place of the Hindus, to end his days there. The journey was long, but I was with him for two days before he died. At times his mind wandered ; but when he spoke, he knew what he was talking of and to whom he was speaking. The moment I stood before him, he recognised me, called me to his side, and asked me to sit. When I had done so, he slowly raised his feeble hands, put them on my head and blessed me. Then he placed one of his hands on my thigh, kept it there for a long time, and counselled me thus : 'Remain where you are. The faith you have embraced keep it to the end. Love all. Never fail to do good, and help your neighbours. Watch the interests of the family. You will suffer. In your sufferings do not forget your God.' Then after a little he said : 'My time is near. I am going to the land of bliss. Go you home.' He was taken to the banks of the holy river to die, and there I saw him draw his last breath."

For about twenty years Tara Babu was pastor of the group of village churches on the great rice plain to the south of Calcutta. Of these churches, the village of Karapukur, on the northern edge of the plain, is the chief station.

About 150 miles to the north of Calcutta, there is a region of extensive swamps, named Gopalgunge. The inhabitants of these dreary marshes, called Chandals, are an illiterate and despised people. Their houses are built on hillocks, and are entirely surrounded by water during the rainy months of the year. Here in 1874 a native missionary built a small thatched house, having determined to preach the Gospel to these people and live among them. "These Chandals," says Mr. Wells, a member of the Indian Civil Service, "were originally a complete Hindu community, consisting of persons of all castes from the Brahman downwards, who, on having the misfortune to be cursed in a body by a vengeful Brahman of unutterable sanctity in Dacca, quitted their ancestral homes, and emigrated bodily to the southern wastes of Fureedpur, Jessore, and Backergunge. There, with great perseverance and toil, they raised, in the centre of the swamps, large hillocks, from twelve to twenty feet high, whereon they built their homesteads in the dry weather, in order to preserve their cattle and goods during the high inundations. In this place they are located to the present day, cultivating the swamps with rice and jute, carrying on the occupations of fishing and bird-catching, varied with mat and basket-making, and the cutting of grass for thatching roofs and for the consumption of their cattle. In the dry weather, they often suffer considerably from scarcity of water. In the rains the whole country becomes inundated; the water rises over ten feet, and leaves their artificial mounds like so many islands in a huge lake. Locomotion then becomes impossible except by boat, while they have to collect their cattle and keep them in their homesteads, feeding them on what fodder they may have stored up during the dry season, and on grass, which, like the rice, grows with the rise of the water, and in appearance very much resembles rice. These cattle have often to remain for weeks standing up to their necks in water; and as their food has to be stored up for them in the homesteads, they are fed on the minimum amount necessary to support existence. Consequently, by the end of the rainy season, they are reduced to skeletons, and very nearly die in the process. Their occupations, and their enforced practice of going about in boats during a great part of the year, have rendered the Chandals a hardy and muscular race, while they present a favourable contrast to their uncursed and therefore contemptuous neighbours in respect of ingenuousness and truthfulness." The Bengali missionary who settled among these people was not a convert of our London Mission, but he was for years with us as a Christian worker in our college at Bhowanipur. He lived among us, and was in various ways closely connected with us. Hence, and because his spiritual history and his work for Christ are so interesting and so encouraging to the friends of Indian missions, he appears in these pages. His case is one in which, as a pamphlet now before me states, there are peculiarities of a special interest. First it shows "the practical relation of the Brahmic theism of Babu Keshub Chunder Sen to Christianity and evangelical missions." It is an instance, too, of an educated gentleman, who had won University honours, and was master of the English language, devoting himself to missionary work in the rude speech of an illiterate and despised community of his own countrymen. The word Chandal indicates their low social position, and commonly carries contempt with it. We have here an instance, also, of a man going forth unconnected with, and receiving no support from, any Missionary Society. He was supported by his fellow native Christians, especially by one, a Bengali merchant, who became a convert of the Free Church Institution in 1850, learned mechanical engineering in England, and fought on our side in the Allahabad Fort during the great rebellion of 1857. The missionary, Mothoora Nath Bose, was ordained in Calcutta, not by the ecclesiastical authorities, or as a missionary of any denomination, but "by a body of European and Bengali missionaries, representing the various Protestant evangelical denominations labouring in Calcutta, who were persuaded that Mr. Bose had received a call from God to labour at Gopalgunge."

In his boyhood he had a deep-rooted prejudice against Christianity, though he knew scarcely anything about it. One day a European missionary came to Jessore, where his home was, and gave him a Gospel. He tore it in pieces before the missionary's face, to show his hatred of the book. The time came for him to leave his home in order to study in one of the Calcutta colleges. He purposed to gain a University degree and devote himself to the legal profession. "The Law" as a profession attracts multitudes of aspiring youths. They see others, once humble students like themselves, who have attained wealth and distinction as lawyers. Why should not they? Before leaving home for the metropolis, the youth went to say good-bye to his Hindu schoolmaster. The teacher warned him against missionary colleges. "If you enter a missionary school," said he, "you will become a Christian." He said this, not because he saw in the student any inclination towards Christianity, rather the contrary; but he knew the youth's inquiring spirit. These words of warning impressed him, and made him afraid of reading and inquiring on the subject of religion. It came about, however, that he did enter a missionary college, that of the Free Church of Scotland, because of the superior instruction he had heard he should obtain there. But he resolved not to pay any attention to the Bible. "At this time I hated Christianity and Christians, though I knew not why I did so." But the spirit within him was ill at ease. He had ceased to worship the Hindu gods "because of their bad character"; and his soul had not any anchorage in religion. He felt his sinfulness. His heart in its gloom and pain cried out for God. Very touching are his own words. "I walked the streets of Calcutta a weary, heavy-laden sinner. Life seemed a burden to me, and myself the embodiment of misery. Anguish of heart had also affected my body. The whole day was spent in sighing and saying within myself: What shall I do? If I die now, I shall surely be turned into hell, for my heart is full of sin." His health gave way under his mental distress, and at one time he meditated ending his misery by suicide. But he was afraid to die, fearing that death would aggravate his misery in the future.

His friends began to notice his wretched looks, and became concerned about him. He spoke at last of his mental trouble to a young friend who was a zealous Brahmo. "He asked me what religion I believed in. I told him that I used to worship the gods of the Hindus, but I had some time ago given up worshipping them. He said, it was a foolish thing to have no religion. Man is a religious being, so he should have a religion. He advised me to accompany him to the Brahmo Samaj (congregation), and hoped that I should embrace the religion of the Brahmos."

He went to the Brahmo worship, and was soothed for a time by the novelty of the assembly and their superior singing. But he soon became as miserable as before. His heart underwent no change. He asked the Brahmo leaders how he should get a better heart, and they advised him to pray for sanctification. He listened to their advice, and night after night prayed: "O God, have mercy upon me; remove my sins, and give me a better heart!" But he found neither peace nor hope; despair and sighing returned. While he was in this condition, the Saviour he shunned met him one day, and talked with him. He listened and wondered, and was comforted. But he did not know that the One whose gracious words fell on his ear was the Lord whose name he still hated. It was on this wise.

One Sunday morning he attended a class meeting of young Brahmos. "Babu Keshub Chunder Sen presided, and read from a book words which seemed to impart life to my dying spirit. While the book was being read, my soul danced within me for joy on hearing the gracious words which it contained." He turned to a friend who sat near him and whispered: "Who is the author of this book?" The friend mentioned the name of Rammohun Roy, the founder of the Brahmo Society. When the class was over, he eagerly asked where he could get a copy of the book, for he thought he had found that morning something that would soothe his troubled soul. The book was out of print; but his acquaintance, yielding to importunity, lent him a copy. "I got the precious treasure, and came home with a heart full of hope, and set at once to read it. I took a hasty breakfast to save time, that I might feast upon the heavenly manna. Sweeter indeed than honey and the honey-comb it seemed to my taste. From morning till night I read it, sitting in my room; and when there was no light there, I came out, and spreading the book towards the west, caught the little light I could, and read on. At this time, a companion came to ask why I had not gone out to walk in his company, as I was accustomed to do. I told him that the cause which detained me at home was in my hand, and that I had at last found that for which my soul thirsted. Rammohun Roy's book, I said, is a precious treasure. He took the book from me, looked at it, and told me that everything in it was to be found in the Bible, that Rammohun Roy was only a compiler." The livelong day the youthful seeker after God had been reading the words of Jesus. In them he had found life.

From that day he began to read the Bible, and found in it food for his hungry soul; his dejected spirit was revived; life was no longer a burden to him. His darkness disappeared at the approach of the true light. Here he found the remedy for the melancholy which had taken possession of him. It never after returned. Holding up the Bible, he would say to all about him: "Is there a book like this book?" To his class-fellows he said: "I have read Milton, Johnson, Addison, and other great authors, but is there any comparison between this book and their works?"

Mr. Bose, after his baptism, made an effort to live in his former Hindu home with his relatives; and it is an interesting fact that they were willing he should do so. The opposition, however, of superstitious neighbours, who regarded the residence of a Christian in a Hindu home as a stain upon the community, soon drove him to seek a home with missionaries.

He longed now to preach the Word of God, which he had found could make a miserable sinner so happy. He went several times with a Christian brother into the interior, sojourned among villagers, and preached to them the glad tidings of salvation. Wherever the preachers went, they found the people glad to receive them and entertain them. These tours produced in his mind such an interest in the poor villagers of Bengal, that he longed to settle among them as a missionary.

Previous to this settlement, Mr. Bose was a professor in our college at Bhowanipur. He heard of the Chandals scattered over the marshes of Fureedpur, as sheep without a shepherd, and he determined to go among them with the word of life, and lead them to the Shepherd of souls. He gave up his professorship, he relinquished all thought of worldly prosperity, and left the city with its advantages to live on a dreary marsh among a people extremely poor and ignorant. Among them he kindled a light which has sent its rays far over those dreary swamps, and guided many to the Saviour.

CHAPTER VIII.

A BENGALI CHURCH AND ITS PASTORS.

ON the road which bounds our mission station northward, there is a neat, substantial building for Christian worship. An inscription on one of the pillars declares it to be the "Bhowanipur Congregational Church." This church is an outcome of educational missionary work. The service is conducted in Bengali; but a sermon in English would be understood just as well by almost all the adult male members of the congregation. I have heard some of them say that for their own use they prefer the English to the Bengali Bible. It is more familiar to them. It is the book from which they first learnt the truths of Christianity. But for the sake of their wives and children, the language of prayer, praise, and teaching, in the church, is their mother tongue.

In the year 1854, when the new institution was opened, the native Christian congregation first obtained a special house for the exercise of worship. They were but few in number, and up to that time had met in the school bungalow on Sundays. But the school was now transferred to the fine new establishment. The bungalow was no longer required as a school; it was pulled down, and the materials were used to build a decent chapel on the old site. The cost of re-building was not more than £40, and the people gave liberally in proportion to their means. Not a farthing was required from the funds of the mission. The building was not new, and certainly not grand. It had slender brick walls and a roof of straw. But the people were pleased with it, even proud of it. No longer to be a school-house for Hindu lads, but a sanctuary for Christian worship, it was set apart for its new use by a special service of devotion. It was a cheering fact, alluded to in the opening service, that in the former school bungalow many of the church members had received their first instruction in the Gospel, and had been brought out of Hinduism into the Church of Christ. Having entered their new sanctuary, the native church adopted a solemn resolution to maintain it for its uses, as far as their means would allow, without charge to the Bengal Auxiliary.

For thirteen years they met and worshipped beneath the roof of straw. Their numbers increased. Youths who had come out from heathenism had, in many cases, left the advantages and comforts of prosperous homes. They possessed nothing, and were dependent on the mission until they had finished their studies and obtained situations. Their circumstances improved. They established homes; and families gathered about them. The desire of the church to become self-supporting grew stronger every day. They desired also a better and more substantial chapel to meet in. At length, in 1867, the foundation stone was laid of the "Bhowanipur Congregational Church." In the same year a terrible cyclone blew off the roof, and injured the slender walls of their chapel, and it ceased to exist just as the new house on a new site was nearly ready for use. Every member of the Church had contributed a month's salary to the building fund. Some gave much more. Generous help was received from European Christian friends. The cost of the new sanctuary was more than Rs. 11,000. The brethren entered their new chapel early in 1868, and one of their first acts as a Church was to write to the committee of the Bengal Auxiliary to the London Missionary Society, requesting them to withdraw the aid they were giving towards the support of the pastor, and to accept the cordial thanks of the Church for the help it had for so many years received from them.

Their first native pastor had been a pupil of the institution. He was an able and faithful man, chosen by the people for the pastoral office. He died young, much loved, and deeply regretted. While the old chapel was lying in ruins, and the new sanctuary was yet unfinished, there were interesting additions to the Church. One Sunday morning the pastor had the pleasure of baptising two young women who, a short time before, were inmates of the Hindu Zenana. They had left their homes with their husbands, Bhogoban Chondro Chaterji and Deno Nath Chowdry. These two men I knew well, and observed their careers in after-life with much satisfaction. The former, while a student, received aid from the mission to enable him to prosecute his studies. He entered the service of Government, and rose to an important and lucrative position as a magistrate. He repaid to the mission the money expended on his education, and has lived a consistent Christian life. The other, Deno Chowdry, has occupied a humbler position. He has been a teacher in the institution for thirty years. A more amiable, unassuming Christian, or a more willing worker, I was not acquainted with—"an Israelite indeed, in whom was no guile."

In March, 1843, a few years after the commencement of the work in Bhowanipur, ten persons partook of the Lord's Supper for the first time. They had been formed into a Christian Church. When the brethren entered their new chapel, in 1868, the adherents were about two hundred, and the communicants seventy-five. This, be it remembered, among classes not easily moved. In the neighbouring institution, many hundreds of youths were receiving instruction in the Scriptures that could make them wise unto salvation. It will be found, I believe, in the day when hidden things shall be brought to light, that in many cases the seed sown in young minds carefully and prayerfully has not perished. In the stress and strain of life, in sorrow and sickness, when the spirit in its dire need looks round for a helper, the truth learnt in early days has become an anchor to the soul, both sure and steadfast. I have known it to be so.

Of that Christian Church I knew five native pastors. Four of them had been pupils of the institution, which they entered as heathen lads.

The first pastor was Surjyo Kumar Ghose. When five youths were baptised in 1851, he was removed from the institution and placed in the Government College at Benares, five hundred miles from Calcutta. But the impressions made by the conversion of his companions were not effaced by his visit to the holy city. He continued to read the Bible in private, and any religious books he could obtain. Returning to Calcutta, he called on our missionaries, who were much pleased with his intelligence and the spirit he showed. But his Christian knowledge was somewhat defective, and his appearance was very youthful. He was therefore advised to study still further the truths of Christianity, but was encouraged by an assurance of willingness to receive him on a stronger evidence of his faith and knowledge. All this was perhaps better proof of the unwillingness of his Christian friends to be in undue haste, than of his unfitness. He went away reluctantly, saying, with grief: "You send me away to idolatry and sin."

He had attained his majority according to Hindu law. Weeks passed away, and he came back several times, earnestly desiring baptism. His father was informed of his visits to the missionaries. Strict orders were given that he should not be permitted to leave the house. He managed, however, to elude his watchers. Then came the scenes so often repeated in these cases, and so distressing to all concerned. It was painful to witness the agony and tears of the father. He begged and entreated his son to change his mind, and return home. For these cruel experiences Hinduism is responsible. There could be no return home in the great majority of such cases, without an absolute denial of the truth. The young man was deeply affected. He was left alone with

BENARES FROM THE GANGES.

his friends for a time. The father's grief changed into fury. A scuffle was heard. Several Christian friends entered the room, suspecting foul play. They found the father apparently trying to strangle his son. He had his hands about the youth's neck, with so tight a grip that his eyes were starting from their sockets, and he could not cry for help. Being released, he fled upstairs. Several attempts were made afterwards to carry him off by force. He had to be removed from the suburbs to the city for security.

A few years after, at the age of twenty-two, he was ordained pastor of the Church. He died after holding that office for fifteen years, much respected both by Hindus and the entire native Christian community of Calcutta. The people placed in the chapel a marble monument to his memory, expressing their affection and grief.

The youth who challenged the genuineness of the document in the Alipore court was Chondro Nath Banerji. He graduated at the Calcutta University, and was for a time pastor of the native Church. At the time of his conversion his father was dead. An only child, he was his mother's pride; and, indeed, there was that in his appearance which any mother might be proud to look upon. He was tall, handsome, erect, and had the fair complexion so much valued among Hindus as a mark of high caste. In his Brahmanhood he took great pride. A worshipper of Kali, he daily visited the temple, bathed in the Ganges, and uttered the holy texts. It was not necessary for him, as it was for many, to learn English for the sake of gaining a livelihood. The revenues of the temple afforded ample support in those days to all belonging to the Haldar families of Kalighat. It is different now. The temple does not yield half so much as it did forty years ago. A significant fact! But so great was his desire to learn English that his mother was persuaded to allow him to attend the institution at Bhowanipur. The result has been told. While he was passing through those wonderful experiences of a newly-awakened soul, he and others with like feelings talked together of these things, but in secret. "What a pity," he says, "I never dared to utter a syllable on the subject, even to my own mother!" One day, when secrecy and indecision had become intolerable, he gave a hint of his feelings and purposes to his young wife. "But I do not think," says he, "she clearly understood my meaning, or her alarm and objections would have been expressed very strongly on the spot. All she did was to run away, ostensibly to look at a procession passing by the house." Possibly the poor girl understood something, and was afraid to understand more.

Soon after, unknown to his friends, he left his Hindu home for ever. His mother's distress and affection, stronger than her shrinking from exposure, led her to follow him to his place of refuge. A carriage drove up to the house, and he heard, to his astonishment, that his mother and grandmother had come to see him. He could not persuade her to go back without him, and finding it impossible to console her, he quietly slipped out of the room. This so much affected her that she seized a knife as if to destroy herself. Just then Mrs. Mullens entered the room. She snatched the knife from her hand, and spoke to her with so much kindness and feeling that she was comforted for a time, and persuaded to return home.

The young wife afterwards joined him, and accepted Christ as her Lord and Saviour. By her gentleness of spirit and manners she won the affec-

REV. TIN KAORI CHATERJI

tion of her Christian friends. Her brother also became a believer. And even the mother, before her death, was well disposed towards the faith her son had embraced.

In this year, 1892, Babu Tin Kaori Chaterji is the pastor of the Church. For several years he had the oversight of our rural Churches south of Calcutta. In that sphere he showed himself an able and faithful minister. He is a man of great modesty, simplicity and amiability, and is a pleasing, persuasive preacher. His pure Bengali, moreover, makes his addresses acceptable to his countrymen, and his high caste as a Hindu secures a respectful hearing. Well may we pray for more of such men for the ministry of the word in India. They have, in many respects, great advantage over the English missionary. They can endure the climate, get to the hearts of the people, and speak their own Bengali as English missionaries, even those best acquainted with the vernacular, cannot be expected to do.

Here is his story as told by himself. "I shall mention three things which, so far as I remember, were used of God in my conversion to the Christian religion. They were, first, the study of the Scriptures ; secondly, prayer ; and thirdly, the godly life of an evangelist, who, after rendering useful and effective service to the London Missionary Society, has gone to his rest.

"First, having been convinced of the folly of idolatry, and the worthlessness of Hinduism to heal the sin-stricken heart, I was led to join the Brahmo Samaj in the hope that I should get peace of mind. I and a few other young men of my native village used to meet privately to talk about the things of God, and to pray to Him to lead us into truth. We were Brahmos, it is true, but we never for a moment thought that we had found what we longed for. We always considered ourselves to be seekers after truth, and used to pray earnestly for Divine guidance. One day, after prayer, we talked among ourselves as to what books we should read in order to find the best moral precepts and an example of a perfect life. The Bible was mentioned as one of the books that would satisfy our desires. I resolved to secure a copy of the Bible. A few days after, I met with a colporteur who was selling his books in the daily market of my village. I induced him to let me have a Bible, and arranged that the price should be paid in two instalments. I brought the volume home, and commenced to read it from the beginning with the greatest avidity. But I was much disappointed, and thought my friends must have made a serious mistake in selecting this book. What I wanted was moral precepts and examples of perfect lives. Genesis, I concluded, could not give me these. When I was thinking of giving it up and selecting some better book, I was advised not to do so hastily, but to read the Psalms and the Gospels, and then decide what to do. Following this advice, I turned to the Psalms. This precious book opened my eyes to see my sinfulness and helplessness. I cried, I abhorred myself, and repented of my sins, but the burden was not removed from my heart. In this state of mind I commenced to read the Gospels, and learnt that Jesus Christ, as the sin-bearer, saved His people from their sins. But how I could be His, how I could come to Him, or if I came, whether He would accept me, were questions that agitated my mind very much. I could not answer them myself, nor was there a missionary near whom I could ask for help.

"Secondly, finding nobody to help me, I took to

prayer. My connection with the Brahmo Samaj, though only nominal, taught me one thing which was a great help to my spiritual life—the power of prayer. I learned that everything might be taken to God in prayer. I asked for guidance and grace. God's name be praised, He gave me light and strength.

"Thirdly, I now fully believed in Jesus, and became a secret follower of the Lord, but could not make up my mind to take the decisive step of openly confessing Him. To confess Christ openly meant with me, as it means with all similarly situated, a tearing asunder of family ties, and complete severance from the Hindu community. In this crisis of my life I was greatly helped by what I saw in the life of a Christian man who came to our village to preach the gospel. I made his acquaintance, and unbosomed my mind to him. For several days he helped me with advice and counsel, and pressed me earnestly to join the Christian Church. I was still halting between two opinions. His example removed my doubts about the Christian community. I was much impressed with his amiable disposition and unfailing courtesy. One thing about him struck me very forcibly: his manner of calling his servant and giving him orders. He called him as one would call a child. Such gentleness towards a Muhammadan servant was altogether a new thing to me. I was accustomed to see menials treated contemptuously; and the only reward often for faithful service was rebuke, unkind words, and sometimes blows. But when I saw a servant treated by his Christian master in this manner, I thought that love must be the ruling principle of the life of the disciples of Jesus, and that I could only be happy in their company. Accordingly I decided to cast in my lot with them. Having made this decision, I came down to Bhowanipur and was baptised."

CHAPTER IX.

A NATION OF FAMILIES.—INDIA'S WOMANKIND.

EVERY nation is made up of its families. But this general statement applies to India as it does not to England. India is emphatically a land of families. In England there are influences at work that scatter the members of households, and the tendency with us is to excessive individualism. We look for this scattering, think it right, or accept it as a necessity. We prepare our sons to leave the family nest, and to go forth and build nests of their own. In India these scattering influences are feared and resisted. They are increasingly felt, but are regarded with sorrow as tending to destroy the ancient system and religion. There the normal state of things is this: that the family should grow, but keep within its own borders, enlarging but remaining one, living under the same roof from generation to generation, going on in the same way as to food, dress, worship, and all in subjection to one head, the eldest male of the family. With him may be younger brothers, sons, nephews, and others, with their wives and children. The family mansion of a man of wealth is like a small colony. I have seen it stated that in a certain house I know of in Calcutta, counting adults and children, there must be about five hundred persons. A large family! This patriarchal system has prevailed in India from a remote antiquity. It reverses our English ideas. The daughters must all go forth: let the sons all stay at home. For a full discussion of the topics of this chapter, I recommend two excellent little books, "The High-Caste Hindu Woman," by a native lady, and "Hindus as they Are," by a Bengali gentleman.

My remarks on the household apply to well-to-do families. Such a family is typical of the national domestic life. The poorer households approach that type as nearly as circumstances permit. A visitor to India, having heard much of the strict seclusion of women, might be surprised to see hundreds of them in the streets of Calcutta. All classes desire the seclusion of their women, but it is a privilege which is out of the reach of the poor. As soon as a man becomes possessed of money, he aims at keeping the female members of his family in seclusion. It is a mark of respectability. If a woman is seen in the streets, it is because she is poor, or because she is not respectable in character. A servant of mine allowed himself the luxury of two wives. His wages were at most sixteen shillings a month. But he also kept a shop. The older woman had to attend to the shop. The younger and favourite wife was kept in genteel seclusion. Ill did she requite his partiality. She decamped with another man, and carried off her husband's savings. The outside world is completely excluded from this inner domestic life. A visitor is admitted only to the outer chambers of his neighbour's house.

The household is the living centre of Hindu society, the stronghold of the Hindu system. It is

A PARSEE WOMAN.

difficult to conceive of Hinduism as existing without its peculiar family life, and its ideas respecting women and the treatment proper for them. Consequently, in Zenana work, missions aim at the very heart of Hinduism. We need not fear lest the statement of this should alarm natives. It is perfectly clear to them. Some are apprehensive and hostile, but the majority recognise what makes for their own interests. They adjust themselves, though slowly, to new ideas. They cannot stand against the force of modern influences. Many there are, moreover, who hail the dawn of a better day. The spirit of pity, fairness, justice towards woman, is growing; but perhaps self-interest is pleading her cause most effectually.

A Hindu family house is so constructed as to turn its back on the outer world. Its outlook is inwards upon itself. Its verandah and doors open on an inner uncovered court. Its outward walls are mostly windowless. The dark, dank passages, the narrow winding staircases, the assignment of distinct quarters to the different sexes,—all this marks the confined, dreary life within. The men's rooms are comparatively light and cheerful. The women's court, which is at the back of the house, is in perpetual gloom. "In a thickly populated city like Calcutta, with its roads densely crowded at all hours of the day, no married female (of the class I am describing) is permitted except in a closed conveyance, either palki or carriage, to leave the house for a single moment to go to that of a neighbour only a few doors from her own. So great is the privacy and punctiliousness with which female honour is guarded in the East."

The prevailing ideas with regard to women give rise to arrangements which are totally unlike those of an English home. Hindu men and women do not take their meals together. It is highly improper in a woman to be seen eating by any male member of the family. The rule is that the women take their meals when the men have finished theirs. The best portions of the food are offered to the men, and the women have what is left. Once in her life the Hindu wife eats with her husband. That is during the marriage ceremonies, never afterwards.

The close Zenana system is strictly enforced in a respectable Hindu family. The young daughter-in-law, the child-wife, newly introduced into the house, is thought to be wanting in manners or modesty, if she is seen in the male quarters of the house. And within the women's apartments she must never speak so loud as to be heard beyond their limits.

Here is an illustration of wifely deportment. A lady missionary had a favourite pupil in a house she visited, an amiable, pleasant young wife. One day the husband was at home when the missionary paid her visit. She was sitting with her pupil when he entered the room. Instantly the wife stood up, and remained standing in silence so long as he was present. He came in several times during the lesson ; she always rose, and stood meekly till he left. It is my belief he wanted to see the English woman. I don't know whether he would feel touched by such a mark of reverence from his wife ; probably not ; he would be quite used to it. Paul says : "Let the wife see that she reverence her husband." But that a wife should be bound to rise to her feet on her lord's appearance, and not feel at liberty to sit down in his presence, this would be thought, even by the most Pauline among us, to be carrying things rather too far.

There are cruel evils connected with this strange family system. There are also some things that must command our admiration. To the latter I refer now, because missionaries are sometimes charged with setting forth only what is monstrous and wicked in these great Oriental systems.

Though the Hindu's wife is chosen for him when he and she are mere children, there are many instances of true and tender conjugal affection. I remember an old pupil of mine speaking to me of his father, whose wife had died. The father was a respectable man, a pleader in one of the Calcutta courts. After the death of his wife he fell into deep despondency. His heart was with the dead. His mind was so unhinged that he could no longer attend properly to his profession, and his affairs were sinking into ruin. "He has never been right," said the youth, "since she died, and he never will be again. He cares for nothing now." A true undying love was there.

Professor Max Müller, in the *Contemporary Review* for August, 1891, gives a story of exceeding beauty and pathos, entitled "An Indian Child-wife." I shall give a brief summary of it in illustration of this present topic. The occasion of the story was the death of Soudamoni Ray, whose husband was a prominent member of the Brahmo Samaj. She was born in 1858, at a village near Dacca, in Bengal. "As an infant she clung to her grandfather, preferring his to all other society. Brought up with tender affection by her father, she was married, at the age of nine, to Kedar Nath Ray, a boy of about twelve. The families they belonged to held prominent positions in Hindu society. When old enough to think of serious subjects, they felt dissatisfied with Hinduism, and, after three years of anxious thought, resolved to give up idolatry and superstitious practices. The husband joined the followers of Ram Mohun Ray. The young wife was in full sympathy with him. They determined to worship the one Father, and Him alone, infinite, eternal, benevolent, all-knowing, omnipotent, the refuge of all. In consequence of this step, they were made outcastes from Hindu society. They were despised, avoided, reduced to poverty, and, at times, almost starving. But they remained steadfast, and were helpers of each other in their religious life.

"Years went on, and they lived quietly in the village which had been the home of their ancestors. Society did not exist for them. No theatres, no concerts, no dinners, no balls. Nature supplied them with all the objects of their admiration, and religion lifted their souls to the sublimest happiness. They well knew the rapture that springs from feeling a Divine presence in everything.

"The young wife watched over their children, and guided them with a firm hand. She clung to her husband, as a creeper clings to a tree, and yet gave him strength. Every morning and evening she prayed with him. Later on in life she conducted domestic worship for her children and servants. When, at last, her health began to fail, though young and happy, she was quite willing to go. In her sickness she did not complain, and her only fear was that she should disturb her husband's slumber, and deprive him of the rest he needed so much. When the end came, she gently murmured: 'Dayamaya,' 'Oh, all Merciful!' Thus passed away a true child-wife, yearning for that Father whom she had sought for, if haply she might feel after Him and find Him."

Some have thought that the story reads too much like an apology for an evil and cruel system. But it is well to be reminded that "it is difficult to remove the veil that covers the happiness and the misery of a Hindu family." The story is not given as an instance of the admirable working of the Hindu marriage system. This couple, early in their married life, ceased to be Hindus. They were persecuted and cast out for abandoning the idolatries of Hinduism in their search for and worship of the one living God. They shaped their domestic life on another and ancient Model familiar to us. "Therefore shall a man leave his father and his mother, and shall cleave unto his wife; and they shall be one flesh."

Again, Hinduism inculcates reverence for parents, respect for elders and teachers. This deference to age, experience, and superior knowledge is a marked feature of Hindu youths. There is a proverb among the natives that "the council of the aged should be accepted for all the practical purposes of life." I have had much to do with the young, and have frequently marked this feature. This is a characteristic, not uncommon in the East, which Christian missions will certainly not seek to destroy, but rather to foster; all the more because there is some danger lest, in the throes of a new and freer life, the nation should lose something of this fine quality. It is in accordance with the teachings of the Bible, and of course we expect to see, and do see, many instances of it in Christian England. But knowing both England and India, there are, I think, in that Eastern land, fewer instances of another kind—instances in which it seems to be thought that years and long experience of life are a disqualification for advising and guiding the young, and that the clearer vision of youth is superior to "old experience," with its wise laws, its cautions, and its antiquated wisdom. The sacredness of motherhood makes itself felt even where the mother may be a secluded occupant of the Zenana, childishly ignorant and superstitious, and the son an English-speaking youth with a Western education and advanced political and social ideas.

As examiner for the Calcutta University, a paper came into my hands, in which a youth gave an account of his journey from his distant home to Calcutta. He was to be absent many days. The journey, partly, I believe, on foot, along lonely roads, partly by river and rail, was probably not free from danger. Before starting he goes into his mother's presence, kneels before her, and asks that her blessing may go with him. The account was given very simply, and, I doubt not, truly. "Honour thy father and mother," is a command impressed on the minds of many Hindu children from their earliest years.

But we are very liable to be carried by partial representations and individual instances to false general conclusions. I could multiply pleasing examples of Hindu life and character. But no greater wrong could be than the position which Hinduism assigns to women. We see this if we go to the highest authority, Manu, the Indian law-giver, whose teachings about women all Hindus accept. Women's nature is so weak that she must be allowed no freedom. The men are commanded to keep the women of their households in constant dependence. "A woman is never fit for independence." "Both day and night a man must keep his wife so much in subjection that she by no means is to be mistress of her own actions." "A woman shall never go out of the house without the consent of her husband, and shall never hold con-

WOMAN PLAYING SITAR.

verse with a strange man, and shall not stand at the door, and must not look out of a window."

She is not only weak, but naturally and incurably prone to evil. To quote here the wise man's estimate of women's character were to give needless pain to every Christian reader, whether man or woman. Confessedly he has said wiser and kinder things.

In religion a woman has no separate existence apart from her husband. She is forbidden to read the sacred books. "No sacrifice, no vow, no fast must be performed by women apart from their husbands; if a wife obeys her lord, she will for that reason alone be exalted to heaven."

His character is to make no difference in her love and consecration to him. "Though destitute of virtue, or seeking pleasure elsewhere, or devoid of good qualities, yet a husband must be constantly worshipped as a god by a faithful wife."

With the above specimens, I hasten to make my escape from these teachings of sacred wisdom.

A son is the blessing beyond all others a Hindu desires. "There is no place for a man [in heaven] who is destitute of male offspring." It became necessary, in view of the awful future, to give some relief to human nature by a modification of this severe law. Hence, if a man is without a son, he may adopt one. If he has a daughter, her son may redeem the soul of his grandfather. That the young Hindu wife should have an intense craving for male offspring is to be expected in the circumstances. In many cases her hope of winning her husband to herself depends on her bearing sons. The sacred laws authorise a husband to supersede his wife by another if she bear only daughters. Should the wife thus introduced be more fortunate, she becomes her husband's favourite, and is likely to be scornful and overbearing. A daughter can bring no good to her parents. She will become the possession of others, body and soul, for life. She brings anxiety and expense, and may cause humiliation. To meet marriage expenses many a father incurs debts which cripple him as long as he lives. The girl must be married within a defined age, to one belonging to the same caste. To find such a husband is often a difficult matter. To have an unmarried daughter who has passed the prescribed age, would bring disgrace and even excommunication.

Notwithstanding all this, in homes where there were sons, I have known of little girls who were the delight of their fathers. I have seen them in our schools until the age arrives for secluding them ; and they show great intelligence, and quickness in learning. Though unwelcome at first, the baby girl wins her way into a father's heart. Nature, the great mother, pleads for her children in the hearts of parents in India as elsewhere.

To us it seems incredible that a child of five should be taught to think of a husband. So it is, however, in India. At that age she begins, under the instruction of an elderly female, a series of prayers and vows having relation to married life. She prays to Siva for a good husband—one like himself, who was devoted to his wife, Durga. In another exercise she asks that her husband may have no second wife to supplant her in his affections. She is taught to curse this possible rival as her enemy, and to ask that the most dreadful evils may befall her.

The Pundita Ramabai mentions an extraordinary marriage, in which a father gave his daughter to a stranger, of whose character he was quite ignorant. Though she speaks of such things as sometimes happening, they surely must be very rare. "The father was on a religious pilgrimage with his wife and two daughters, one nine, the other seven years of age. They had stopped in a town to rest for a day or two. The father one morning was bathing in the sacred river Godaveri, when he saw a fine-looking man coming there to bathe also. The father inquired of the man who he was and whence he came. On learning that he was a widower, he offered him his little daughter in marriage. In an hour or so everything was settled. Next day the marriage took place, and the little girl was handed over to the stranger, whose home was nearly nine hundred miles away." Next day the father pursued his pilgrimage with a light heart.

The life of a little girl while with her parents in a well-to-do household is often bright and joyous. She is petted and indulged, is unfettered in her movements, and is not troubled with learning. What a change for her when the day comes for removing her to the family of her future husband! She is brought to be confined for life in the dark and cheerless rooms of the women's court, and to take the humblest position in the household. There are undoubtedly mothers-in-law who are kind and affectionate to the little girls given up to their control. Sometimes a woman about to part with her child goes to the future mother-in-law and entreats her with tears to be kind to the little girl. Surely she does not always appeal in vain to the womanly heart! But in many a case the child's lot is hard work without a word of praise, and without the pleasures and encouragement a child ought to have. Of this inner domestic life, so screened from observation, I cannot speak as of "that which I have seen with my eyes." I shall give words written by a Hindu woman, which pathetically describe the too common experiences of the child-wife.

"If the work is well done it is silently accepted words of encouragement and praise from the elders being regarded as spoiling children, and demoralising them; the faults of the little ones are often mistaken for intentional offences, and then the artillery of abusive speech is opened on them. In such distress, the only consolation they can find is in silent tears."

How different is the prospect of a young English girl, of respectable family, who is preparing to be united in marriage to the young man she loves! She looks forward to be mistress in her home. She will have her husband and her house all to herself. She will arrange everything to suit her own taste, and his also, for the two are agreed. They will be everything to each other; and while she serves her husband in his home, she will reign as a queen in his heart!

Enlightened Hindus are themselves ashamed of some things in their social system. Yet they may not like that these should be pointed out. As Max Müller has said, their feeling is—"Let us alone, and we shall right these things ourselves in time." Great and beneficent changes have come about among them, but certainly not by leaving them alone.

Wrong done to woman brings its Nemesis. The family system of India is not favourable to the production of that wedded happiness of which there are many instances in Christian homes, and which even the old heathen poet Homer so well understood, and so finely depicted :—

> " Since nought is lovelier on the earth than this,
> When in the house one-minded to the last
> Dwell man and wife—a pain to foes, I wis,
> And joy to friends—but most themselves know their own bliss."

CHAPTER X.

A WELL-SPRING.

THE enclosure in which the Calcutta cathedral stands is a peaceful and attractive spot. There is the brightness and beauty of flowers; there is the relief of deep shadow under wide-spreading trees. In a corner of this quiet garden stood a cottage occupied by a native Christian family. The man had charge of the cathedral library. The wife, Bosonto Kumari Singh, with whom I often exchanged a word as I passed her cottage door, carried my thoughts back to the devoted woman whose name is associated with the beginnings of missionary work for the elevation of the women of India.

Mrs. Mullens was a loving, lovable, and attractive woman, and when she died there was genuine sorrow in many hearts. I enjoyed her acquaintance a few months only, but could not fail to notice one characteristic which she possessed in an unusual degree. In her mind, interest gathered around every human being she had to do with. It was so even with regard to the poorest natives about her, heathen or Christian. She spoke, with simple, unaffected concern, of them, their families, and their affairs. Thus, as the spontaneous outcome of her own nature, without thinking of any command, she "honoured all men." The law was written on her heart. They were all, like herself, human beings, the sons and daughters of the same Father. So spiritual was she, and yet so thoroughly human in all the common humanities of every-day life! Everybody felt the strong fascination of her rare and radiant personality. Especially was her womanly heart drawn out towards the women of India. She felt deeply their needs and sorrows.

When I first reached Calcutta she was absent in England. She wrote to her friends in India: "Oh, how I love mission work! Missions are a passion with me. And I bless God that I have learned from my dear father to labour on contentedly without visible success. I shall go back quite cheerfully to my Bengali women, among whom I can hope to sow only the merest germs of truth."

Early in 1861 she returned to Calcutta. There had been a decided advance in native opinion on the subject of female education, and she found unexpected openings into a new sphere of Christian work—the instruction of Hindu ladies in their own homes. In this department scarcely anything had been done. In the Indian Missionary Statistics for 1861, compiled by Dr. Mullens, there is no mention of Zenana pupils. She gained access to several houses in our neighbourhood, and the work soon grew on her hands. It was a great advantage that she was living under the same roof with her widowed mother, Mrs. Lacroix, who was in full sympathy with her aims.

"Now, Hannah," said her mother, upon her return

to India, "give yourself to your schools and Zenanas as you wish. I will set you free from all household duties. That shall be my share in the work."

She accepted to the full her mother's offer, and became absorbed in this Christian service.

But she gave offence to some of her acquaintance. Europeans in India are much given to pleasant evenings in the society of friends. They dine late, then adjourn to the drawing-room. There they pass the hours enjoying the breeze from swinging puṇkahs, conversing, listening to music, sipping tea which makes them hot, and then taking ices to make themselves cool. Mrs. Mullens was a woman whose society was much sought after. It had been hoped that after her return to India she would be present at many such social gatherings. But she resisted entreaties, and had to brave reproaches. She said to friends: "Do not be offended with me. I could enjoy your company. But there is so much to be done. My work needs all my time."

It was as if she felt that the end was near, and she must do with her might what she had to do. Before the close of that same year of her return she died, at the age of thirty-five. Suddenly was she removed, and by a pathway of extreme agony. Her simple, childlike nature showed itself in her last prayers for relief. Folding her hands, as a little child, between the paroxysms of anguish, she would say: "Please, heavenly Father, please help me!" Her Father heard her. He said: "Come to Me, My child," and released her spirit from the suffering body.

The woman at the cottage near the cathedral, a Hindu widow, thirty-two years ago, troubled in spirit and in quest of peace, came to Mrs. Mullens, and was led to the knowledge of Christ. She is a woman of faith and prayer; for many years she has been engaged in visiting Zenanas, and has earnestly worked for the salvation of her countrywomen. A knowledge of native medicines, and familiarity with sickness, give her readier access to the women, and make her visits welcome. For kindness I had shown her, I do not remember when or how, she was much concerned about my leaving India, and brought to the superintendent of the Zenana work a whole month's salary towards a testimonial of goodwill. She gives the following simple story of a long struggle, and of rest found at last in Christ.

"I was married in my ninth year. In my twelfth year I became a widow. It is a great misfortune for a Hindu girl to become a widow at such a tender age. I was plunged into two of the deepest sorrows that can befall one—grief for the loss of my mother, and also the sorrow of widowhood. I had not the consolation of going to my father for comfort, now that my mother was dead; he was still living, but the double blow of my mother's and my husband's death had driven him mad. He left me at home, and went to live at Benares. From that time my mind became unsettled. My time was spent at my own home and at the houses of my father-in-law and my uncle. In this way another twelve years passed.

"I became a Christian when I was twenty-four years of age. During the twelve years of my widowhood, and while yet a Hindu, I made pilgrimages to hundreds of shrines, saw many places, and became familiar with the various religious observances of the

Hindus. I performed many vows, but gained no inward peace, and only wasted my money.

"The worship of gods of clay and stone, gods which man's hands have fashioned, can never be the true worship. When I fully understood this, I made four pilgrimages to Tarkessor, and fasted, that I might come to know Him whom I had not found by meditation and abstraction of the mind from earthly objects.

"There are two special fasts—one for three days, during which not a drop of water can be taken by a widow, and another for five days, during which a little water or milk may be drunk. For my own benefit and that of others, I went to Tarkessor, fasted, and brought away charms. My relations, and the people of my village, seeing my frequent fasts, became angry with me, and said: 'Why do you fast so often, and afflict your body? It was written on your forehead (in your fate) that you would be fatherless and motherless, and become a widow, and that has come upon you; then what is the good of afflicting yourself?'

"One day, when our family priest was bathing the god in the temple, I was preparing rice, flowers, etc., for worship. He said to me: 'Do poojah (worship), make vows, and you shall certainly be blessed. Do not afflict your body any more. Why do you take so much trouble?' My answer was: 'Because I want to know God.' He further said: 'If you think truly, and really wish to see Him, then I solemnly declare you *will* find Him.' Soon after I left my father's house and went to my father-in-law's. One day, while there, I saw a young boy sitting on the roof, and reading

A CALCUTTA BUNGALOW.

some of the Psalms of David aloud. I heard these words: 'Hear, O Lord, when I cry with my voice: have mercy also upon me, and answer me. When Thou saidst, Seek ye My face; my heart said unto Thee, Thy face, Lord, will I seek. Hide not Thy face far from me; put not Thy servant away in anger: Thou hast been my help; leave me not, neither forsake me, O God of my salvation' (Ps. xxvii. 7-9) On hearing these words, I thought to myself: 'Perhaps this is the true religion,' for the words went to my heart. I heard, too, that some young men in Dr. Duff's College were intending to become Christians, and also that arrangements had been made in some quarters to receive and train young women who wished to become Christians. Again I went to visit my uncle at Behala. My real object was to search out the truth. There I met a young man called Raj Krishto, who was studying in the Bhowanipur Institution. I asked him whether there was a girls' school as well as a boys' at Bhowanipur. He replied: 'There is a girls' school, and a number of teachers, and they are very respectable.' Learning this, I left Behala, and went to another uncle's house on pretence of bidding him good-bye before going to live in Benares. When I had been there a day or two, they hired a conveyance to take me away. They also sent a maid-servant with me, and told her to accompany me as far as my father-in-law's house at Barahanagur. I got into the carriage, and when we came near to Bhowanipur, I said to her: 'It is a long way; I know the driver, he will take me; you can go home.' I gave her an old sari and two pice, whereupon she agreed, saying: 'I left my work unfinished to come with you;

if you will kindly spare me, I will go.' She then left me, When the carriage came in front of the L.M.S. Institution, I called to the coachman to stop, and said to him: 'I have friends here; I am going to see them.' I then jumped out of the carriage, and not waiting to say anything more, went to the mission house. I was soon taken to see Mrs. Mullens, and after some conversation with her, the ayah took me to see the girls. I learned to read Bengali, and soon began to go out with Mrs. Mullens to work in the Zenanas. From that time to this, thirty years, I have never ceased to labour for God. Christ said to the woman of Samaria, 'He that drinketh of the water that I shall give him shall never thrist; but the water that I shall give him shall become in him a well of water springing up into eternal life.' I am joyfully offering the water to others. I thank God that He has spared me so long to labour for Him."

CHAPTER XI.

STREAMS THAT MAKE GLAD.

MAY meetings in Calcutta, with the thermometer at 100° in the shade, are far from agreeable. At Bhowanipur a commodious Zenana Home had been built at a cost of more than thirty thousand rupees, and the opening meeting in 1882 was held in the burning month of May. Many European friends came to manifest their interest in our work. In India, one way of showing sympathy with fellow-workers in the good cause, is to sit for hours in a crowded room, in a temperature that would be utterly overpowering but for punkahs swinging overhead. Such are May meetings in Calcutta!

At this gathering it was noticed how great an advance in female education had been made in Calcutta within a few years. Connected with the different missionary societies there were six establishments such as the one now opened. All of them had come into existence, or to their present expanded form and increased usefulness, within the preceding fifteen or twenty years. Each of them was connected more or less directly with a circle of schools and Hindu homes into which it was pouring Christian influences and Christian instruction. The number of day scholars and Zenana pupils connected with these institutions was 4,428.

There is a vital connection between this work in the Zenanas and our educational efforts in schools and colleges for boys and young men. The hundreds we have in these institutions come from the homes visited by our lady missionaries. The girls and women are their mothers, wives, and sisters. A missionary was teaching a girl in a Zenana, and had just given her a Bengali tract, when her brother came in from school. The lad took it up, and said: "You need not give her that; I have it. The sahib gave it to me yesterday at school. It's a very good tract, and I wish you would give her one every week; then I could read them too. You may be sure I will take good care of them."

Here is a vivid picture of Zenana life. "Our pupils who are interested in some kind of work anticipate our visit, and have all in readiness when we go. The picture before us then is brighter than the one we see when we visit a house for the first time, and hear the confession of a number of women, that none of them can read, or do any kind of needlework. The frail, languid look of many of them, who rarely breathe the fresh air, care nothing for the outside world, and know nothing of the beauties of nature, or even the appearance of the town they live in, and with minds that seem almost dead to pure influences; all quarrelsome and inactive, surrounded by petted and spoiled children in close and dirty rooms, this is only a very little of what we witness every day in their houses."

These visits bring rays of brightness to cheerless

lives, and comfort to sorrowing hearts. A Bengali gentleman met one of our ladies, and said to her: "I wish you would come and see my wife. She is in great trouble, and your words always comfort her." The woman had recently parted with her two little girls. They had been married, and, as the custom is, made over for life to their mothers-in-law and future homes. Their mother would not be comforted. The separation is so total and final, it is almost like death.

JINRICKSHA FOR ZENANA VISITOR.

One of our missionaries was asked to visit a young mother, who had passed through a time of great sorrow. Within ten days, her three children died of cholera. For some months she was quite inconsolable, and did nothing but grieve for the dead. Her husband was much concerned for her, and, sorrowing himself, endeavoured to divert her mind from its sorrow. He asked her if she would learn needlework, if she would learn to read English, if he should ask an English lady to visit her. She consented, and "I was asked," says one of our missionaries, "to teach her. At first she was very depressed, and the mention of her little ones brought tears to her eyes. Gradually, however, she began to brighten up, and take real interest in her lessons. My visits made her think of other things; and I was pleased to see how warmly she welcomed me. Once I could not go on the right day, so she sent a servant to see whether I was ill, or what was the reason of my absence. I asked her if she would come and see me at the 'Zenana House.' The idea pleased her, and one afternoon her husband brought her in a closed carriage, and they spent about an hour and a half with us. On leaving she pressed my hands, and said: 'Will you promise always to love me, and never forget me?' It is a great privilege thus to be allowed to bring a little brightness and comfort into such homes as this." No wonder if in such a case the stricken one clings to the Christian sister who has led her from her grief to "think of other things," and, above all, has whispered to her a new, sweet, wonderful hope.

It is not easy for an English mother with Christian hopes to realise the desolateness and despair of the young Hindu mother who loses her babe. The feeling of her heart is: "Farewell, farewell, for ever farewell." "In such hours of supreme grief, Hinduism has no word of comfort or hope. The Hindu says: 'We bring no memories of the past with us; we carry none with us into the next life.'" Her loss, she feels, is utter, complete, final. It is as if a precious jewel had slipped from your hand and sunk into the depths of the ocean. Yet the comparison is inadequate. "For what is a jewel, the most precious," said a mother who had lost children, "in comparison with the babe who has put its little arms about your neck?" What, then, must it be to be pointed to Him who "shall gather the lambs with His arm and carry them in His bosom," to hear a friend she has learnt to love and trust, say: "Do not weep as if there were no hope; your child is not lost; it is in the keeping of that Jesus I tell you of. He will put it into your arms again; believe in Him"!

A few years ago I went to hear a lecture on "Women in Bengal twenty-five years ago and now." A large hall in the "City College" was crowded with English-speaking young men. Most of them were Hindus, some were Brahmos. The majority were students. I noticed a native gentleman moving about the room, and found he was the principal of the college. Presently he came up to me, shook hands, and told me he was an old scholar of mine. Twenty-nine years before he had been a pupil of our institution at Bhowanipur. The lecturer just then entered, and was received with loud cheering. He was a well-known lawyer of the city, and a member of the native Christian Church. Hindu students, aiming to distinguish themselves by their mastery of English and acquaintance with English literature, feel a patriotic pride in one of their own people who is a match for any Englishman in the use of our tongue. He reflects credit on them. These two gentlemen came up to me, and pressed me to take the chair. The over-crowding of the room gave rise to much shouting and confusion. The lecturer's clear, strong voice soon reduced the audience to silence.

As a Christian man before that vast audience, he began by ascribing praise to God for the blessed change the last twenty-five years had witnessed in the condition of women. The Government Educational Report of twenty-five years ago showed about 500 females under instruction. In the latest report the number was 80,000, increased now probably to 100,000. Fifteen girls' schools were reported under inspection at the earlier date. The number had grown to two thousand.

The standard of education at first was simply reading and writing. But the education of females had so pressed forward that the University was compelled to open its doors to admit them to its degrees. There are now young lady B.A.s and M.A.s in Calcutta. A number had devoted themselves to the study of medicine, and one year a girl stood at the head of all the candidates, male and female, for the M.B. degree. An interesting circumstance was mentioned. There were two Brahmo women, mother and daughter. They became believers in Christ, and professed their faith. They began to study, and went up together to the matriculation examination of the University. The daughter passed, the mother failed. She went up again, and again failed. A third time she presented herself, and passed. Then she left her daughter to go on alone to the higher examinations.

I was present at a convocation of the Calcutta University. His Excellency the Governor-General of

India, Lord Dufferin, presided. The large hall was crowded for the most part with students who had successfully passed examinations for the degrees of M.A. and B.A., and had assembled to receive their diplomas. Many professors, too, of the various Colleges affiliated to the University, and, of course, the whole body of examiners, were present. It was altogether a male gathering, with the exception of two or three ladies interested in the ceremony, and still another exception to be noticed presently.

This conferring of degrees is a protracted, monotonous, and weary business, specially trying in that sultry climate. Of the hundreds of students, every one receives his parchment separately, with a form of words repeated to each one, "charging him solemnly to act worthily," etc., etc. I think it was the Vice-Chancellor who discharged this function.

His Lordship was seated in an easy chair, in a conspicuous position. The form of words repeated hundreds of times became an indistinct mumble-jumble. The company in that august presence was still and orderly; nothing was heard but the rustling of academic gowns, as the students went up by batches to be charged and diplomaed. The heat was oppressive, and, after a time, it became evident that His Excellency the Governor-General was——asleep in his Vice-regal seat! And no wonder. How long he had slept I cannot say, when the heavy silence, together with his Lordship's repose, was suddenly broken by a ringing cheer from every part of the hall—a cheer so hearty that it might have come from British instead of Hindu throats. His Lordship opened his eyes, and saw standing before him two young girls, dusky beauties of Hindustan. They had come to receive their diplomas for the B.A. degree. His Lordship slept no more. At the close of the convocation, he walked up to the young ladies and shook hands with them. One of these girls I knew well. Her father, of the Brahman caste, had in his young days been a pupil of mine, when preparing to be a Christian preacher. She was married, and her husband was one of my students. He with me, and she at an institution for girls in Calcutta, were preparing at the same time for the B.A. examination. She was ready a year before her husband, but in deference to the wishes of friends, and from her own sense, I suppose, of what was becoming in a wife, she would not go up before her lord. She waited till he was ready, and they appeared at the same examination, and received their diplomas on the same day. What if she had passed and he had failed! Would it not have been a blow to the incipient work of female education in India—a work which has been opposed by strong prejudice? Had there been many instances of this kind among the women, it might have been argued, as of yore: "They shall despise their husbands in their eyes." The social order would be inverted by the women coming to the top. So female education might have been stopped by the combined and resolute action of the husbands, and the old order of things restored. We may imagine a decree going forth again in the East, as in the days of old, that "all the wives shall give to their husbands honour, both to great and small."

CHAPTER XII.

ENGLISH SANCTUARIES.—AFFECTING MEMORIALS.

THERE are two English chapels in Calcutta connected with the London Mission. The smaller of the two is pleasantly situated on the banks of the river, in a quiet suburb called Hastings. The suburb lies on the western edge of the wide grassy plain I have already described. The "Maidan," with its long green reaches, its avenues and clusters of trees, separates Hastings from the dust and din and Oriental smells of the great city.

The memory of the pretty little chapel at Hastings is dear to me. There for many years, in addition to my missionary work in the Bhowanipur Institution, I ministered to a congregation of Europeans and Eurasians. I can remember in that little congregation some of the best Christians I have ever known. It was fluctuating and changing, as all European society in India is, and was strikingly diverse in its composition. I ministered to seafaring men from England and Scotland, to pilots who brought ships up the dangerous Hoogley, to commanders and engineers of steam-boats that plied on the great Indian rivers, to officers of the Army Commissariat, to soldiers who occasionally dropped in from the neighbouring Fort William. I can remember men who had been at the storming of Delhi when it was held by the Mutineers in 1857, and men who had fought among the mountains of Afghanistan, and some who had done battle with the warlike Sikhs before the conquest of the Punjab. There were women who had been shut up in the Residency at Lucknow when the little garrison was besieged by some sixty thousand Sepoys. I had to do with military officers who had risen from the ranks in stirring times, and whose soldierly training had helped to make fine men of them. They were men of simple and devout character, upright, respectful, open-handed. When I was sitting in their houses, they would tell me some of their experiences. One had served in that final Sikh war, after Lord Dalhousie's remarkable utterance at a farewell banquet in Calcutta, before he left for the north-west: "Unwarned by precedent, uninfluenced by example, the Sikh nation has called for war, and on my word, sir, they shall have it with a vengeance." Those words doomed the Punjab to conquest and annexation. Another of my congregation told me of a remarkable escape he had at the time of the Mutiny. He was in charge of native troops, and heard that the spirit of rebellion had got among his men. The course commonly taken by mutinous regiments was to shoot their officers, and then march off to join the main body of the rebels. One day, on leaving his bungalow, my friend was confronted by one of his own Sepoys, who raised his musket and levelled it at him. With great self-possession he called out to

HASTINGS CHAPEL, CALCUTTA.

the Sepoy: "Ground arms!" The man was so used to the word of command from him, that he obeyed instantly. And then he answered like a machine to all that followed. I cannot vouch for the correct order or accuracy of the phrases I use. "Stand at ease!" "Shoulder arms!" "Wheel about!" "March!" So he marched the intending murderer off the ground. Then going into his bungalow he called his wife and children together, hastily collected a few things they could easily carry, and then betook themselves to the jungle for hiding. There was a native who knew their hiding-place. He dared not, and indeed could not, protect them; but he said: "I'll not betray you, and I'll see that you are fed." Every day for many days the Englishman found food placed in a spot agreed upon between the two; so he and his wife and children were kept alive until they could join friends, except that one little child died through insufficient food or exposure.

These "war-broken soldiers," and men of the free winds and waves, also wives and widows residing in the quiet settlement, met together in the little chapel on the banks of the "ancient river" to "sing the Lord's song in a strange land." On the walls of the chapel are memorial tablets in grateful recollection of missionaries who "spoke unto them the word of God," and Christian friends who helped them in other ways—Mundy, Parker, Payne, Mrs. Mullens—whose work in the Sunday school was much valued and blessed, and Mrs. Slater, who, on her homeward voyage, died at sea, and was buried in the Bay of Cadiz.

Dhurrumtollah is the name of one of the busiest thoroughfares in Calcutta. Roughly speaking, it divides the European from the native city. On this road, and so in the heart of the city, stands Union Chapel, the older and larger of the two English sanctuaries connected with the mission. Bishop Heber has somewhere spoken of Union Chapel as one of the simplest and chastest Christian buildings he had seen in India. In the chapel are monuments in memory of many early missionaries of the Society. Among them the following affecting memorial tells a sad tale as to the fearful nature of the climate of Lower Bengal. The reader will be struck with the line of figures showing their ages at the time of death.

"TO THE MEMORY OF THE FOLLOWING MISSIONARIES
OF THE
LONDON MISSIONARY SOCIETY,
WHO HAVING FAITHFULLY LABOURED IN THE
SERVICE OF CHRIST IN THIS COUNTRY,

DIED

WHILST PROSECUTING THEIR IMPORTANT WORK.

Nathaniel Forsyth arrived in India in 1798. Died February, 1816	Aged 47 years.
Robert May arrived in 1812. Died August 12th, 1818	Aged 30 years.
J. D. Pearson arrived in 1817. Died October, 1831	Aged 41 years.
Robert Hampson arrived in 1819. Died September 1st, 1820	Aged 25 years.
William Bankhead arrived in 1822. Died October, 1822	Aged 23 years.
Joseph Warden arrived in 1822. Died January 8th, 1826	Aged 25 years.
James Adam arrived in 1828. Died April 21st, 1831	Aged 27 years.
James Robertson arrived in 1826. Died June 15th, 1833	Aged 30 years.
Thomas Higgs arrived in 1830. Died December 3rd, 1832	Aged 24 years.

'Now Faith is the Substance of things hoped for,
The evidence of things not seen. For by it the Elders
Obtained a good report. These all died in faith,
Not having received the promises,
But having seen them afar off,
And were persuaded of them, and embraced them,
And confessed that they were strangers.'

THIS TABLET
Is erected by Christians of different denominations
As an expression of respect for the
MEMORY OF BRETHREN
Who were esteemed worthy to labour and die in the
MISSIONARY FIELD."

The London Missionary Society was founded in 1795, and its first missionary to India was Nathaniel Forsyth. The beginnings of the London and Baptist Missions lie close together, like the well-springs of our two great Indian rivers, the Ganges and the Brahmapootra. Cradled near each, in a valley among the northern mountains, the streams take their separate courses to fertilise the burning plains.

But the beginnings of the Baptist Mission in Bengal are connected with a name which is known and revered throughout Christendom, the name of William Carey. The story of the struggles and sufferings and final successes of that strong, patient man is lifted into observation, and stands conspicuous like one of the mountain peaks which overlook the plains on which he passed his life. In 1892, the centenary year of the Baptist Missionary Society, this man and his labours have been subjects of earnest discourse in every Baptist chapel in the land. There have been great gatherings, and the hearts of multitudes have felt afresh the claims and the glory of the Lord's saving work.

The names of the majority of the Lord's workers in mission lands and elsewhere are not widely known ; and soon they pass altogether into oblivion. They are quite forgotten among men. But the Lord is mindful of them. The London Missionary Society's work is widely spread over India, and has been greatly blessed. The Christian community connected with the mission numbers about sixty-three thousand. There are several hundreds of native preachers, and about seventy European missionaries, male and female. About twenty-seven thousand children are receiving Christian education in our schools. The commencements of this great work lie out of sight, and are known only to those who care to search for such details. Mr. Forsyth, the Society's first missionary, proceeded to the small station of Chinsurah, about twenty miles above Calcutta, on the river Hoogley. Doubtless there were good reasons for avoiding the British capital. His presence there might attract hostile attention from the Government, and lead to the suppression of his mission. A circumstance which occurred only the year before his arrival is illustrative of the period. An American vessel reached Calcutta having on board four young men who were on their way to join Mr. Carey at Maldah as indigo planters and missionaries. In order to prevent disappointment, before leaving England they had taken counsel with old Anglo-Indians friendly to missions, and "had determined not to land at the English capital, and fling themselves into the lion's den." When the vessel anchored in the Hoogley, the little company descended the ship's side, placed themselves in a river boat, and made their way to the Danish settlement of Serampore, beyond the reach of English law. Serampore was, as Mr. Kay remarks in his "Christianity in India," a sort of Alsatian receptacle for outcasts of all kinds. And it was believed that "the the most perilous and pestilential of all suspected persons at that time in India, the missionary of the Gospel," might lie there without molestation. The Government, on hearing of the arrival of the missionaries, became alarmed and indignant, and it was feared for some time that the Governor-General would demand their extradition. Though Chinsurah was not beyond the reach of English law, Mr. Forsyth would be less under observation and less liable to molestation than at the capital. For fourteen years he lived and worked there, alone, without sympathy and in the midst of a people wedded to a hostile creed. Those who have had experience of Lower Bengal, the oppressiveness of its sultry, damp climate, the deadening influence of isolation, and the opposition of the heathen to the Christian worker, will understand the difficulty of such a position, and that it would be hard for a man so placed not sometimes to lose heart and hope. The coming of Mr. Forsyth to India was the fragmentary outcome of a remarkable but abortive attempt to enter Bengal as a mission field. At the head of that enterprise was the devoted Robert Haldane. I shall quote the Rev. C. B. Lewis's interesting account of that attempt and its failure. "Mr. R. Haldane became impressed with the spiritual destitution of Bengal, and resolved to devote himself and all the resources God had given him to the work of its evangelisation. He inherited the estate of Airthrey near Stirling, was most happily married, and for ten years had occupied his property, when an all-controlling desire to live for Christ and for man compelled him to exchange a life of elegant retirement and affluent ease for one of vigorous, self-sacrificing, Christian activity. In his project of a mission to Bengal he found a band of devoted men ready to co-operate with him. Especially the Revs. Messrs. Innes, Bogue, and Ewing, who were eminent for Christian usefulness then, and whose after-lives abundantly fulfilled their early promise, undertook to share with him the apostolic labours to which he was eager to consecrate himself. The combined contributions of no association or society were desired or needed for the support of their mission. Mr. Haldane sold Airthrey, and the proceeds were all available for the maintenance of himself and his companions in their noble undertaking. They proposed to establish themselves at Benares, where, with a staff of printers, catechists, and schoolmasters, they would carry forward the preaching of the gospel, the translation and publication of the Scriptures, the Christian instruction of the young, and every other department of Christian effort which the providence of God might render possible and desirable. Probably about thirty persons were ready to employ themselves in these various labours in cooperation with Mr. Haldane.

It was a truly magnificent instance of Christian devotedness! Mr. Haldane kept back nothing; but would consecrate his large property and himself also to the propagation of the gospel in India. Nor was this a mere project! As far as the steps necessary to carry out the design could be taken, he took them. He then sought to obtain the sanction of the Board of Directors and of the British Government. Mr. Dundas, then at the head of Indian affairs, was visited, and in repeated private interviews was made acquainted with the plan, and his acquiescence in it was entreated. On the 29th December, 1796, the Court of Directors was petitioned by the intending missionaries to grant its consent to the enterprise. A reply was soon given to the effect that weighty and substantial reasons induced the court to decline compliance with their request.

The missionaries did not readily abandon the hope of success. New directors were to be elected in April, 1797. They resolved to await the formation of the new court, and then to renew their application. In May the intending missionaries again addressed the Board, urging them by every motive of policy and duty to review their decision. They appealed to all the principles likely to operate upon the human mind: to their justice, their interests, their humanity, their love of literature, their philanthropy, their religion, their hopes and fears for this world and the next. The petition concludes thus: "The favour we ask of you, gentlemen, is leave to go out to Bengal, and protection there, while we demean ourselves as peaceable subjects of the Government and good members of the community."

The petition was sent to the court, supported by letters from many hundreds of clergymen and ministers of England, Scotland, and Ireland, earnestly urging their compliance with the request made to them. The petition and letters were received, and much more deliberate attention was given to them than to the former application.

The result was the same. Permission was refused. One director is reported to have said that "he would rather see a band of devils in India than a band of missionaries."

Mr. Forsyth was one of the devoted men intending to go out to India with Mr. Haldane. "When that enterprise failed, he still persisted in his purpose to labour in Bengal. He was indefatigable in his attempts to do good as he had opportunity, and he supported himself by his own property."

Here we have the humble but noble beginning of the London Missionary's work in India.

CHAPTER XIII.

THE CITY.

CALCUTTA lies along the eastern bank of the Hoogley. There is a road which starts eastward from the water's edge at the north end of the city, and, sweeping round in an irregular curve, joins the river again about seven miles lower down the stream. This road embraces the entire city, and is called the Circular Road.

The ancient Ganges, in its course towards the sea, throws off a branch called the Bhagaruttee. This stream flows south past Murshedabad, once the capital of Bengal, and past Berhampur, a great military station in bygone days. A little lower down, the river sends off a second branch, the Jellinghee. Still further on it parts with a third offshoot, the Matabhanga. These three daughters of Mother Ganges—Gunga Ma!—approach each other as they flow south through Lower Bengal. From the place where their waters mingle, the stream is the Hoogley.

A discrepancy sometimes appears in the numbers given as the population of Calcutta. At one time it is said to be 800,000, at another time 400,000. The

HARE SCHOOL AND RESIDENCY COLLEGE.

larger number includes the population on the outer side of the great Circular Road. The smaller number means the people between the river and the road, the proper boundaries of the city.

What a medley of races and nationalities, and religions and customs lies within these boundaries, "out of every nation under heaven"! Many-tongued is Calcutta. How different in its sameness is an English town from our Eastern capital, with its varieties of human feature, speech, colour, costume! An evening drive on the Esplanade is a good opportunity to see many of the earth's nationalities. For then well-to-do Calcutta, Western and Oriental, goes out to take the air in open carriages.

European and native Calcutta are separate. The Viceroy's Palace, the magnificent range called Writer's Buildings, the Town Hall, the High Court, the General Post Office, the Museum, the English shops on fine wide roads, the Chowringhee Road, with the quiet, respectable streets that lie behind it,—these all form a whole, and are not far from the river. Further inland and to the north is the great native town. There is, however, much overlapping and interspersion of the European and native elements.

The Chinaman in his loose blouse and wide trousers, with his square yellow face and quiet, self-possessed demeanour, seems to be everywhere. Between the chief European quarter on the south and the native town on the north there is a street lined with boot and shoe shops, kept by Chinamen. Our best shoes, for church and sitting-room, were got from Chinamen. They are more expensive than the Bengali-made articles, but they wear three or four times as long. The Chinaman does not praise his goods, and press them on you. He does not seem anxious to sell. He tells you his price when asked, and goes on with his work. You may take the articles or leave them. Not that he is insolent, but he is a man of few words, and he cannot waste time in haggling. If you deal regularly with a Chinese shoemaker, you acquire a respect for him, and feel that your feet are safe in his hands. The Bengali salesman in the bazar runs after you, pours out floods of words in praise of his wares, asks a high price, and takes a third of what he asks. You may find that you have bought almost as much brown paper as leather.

English ladies resident in Calcutta who cannot afford the high prices asked at English shops are compelled to visit native markets such as the Burra (great) Bazar. They find shopping there a rough experience. They have to go prepared for din, and dirt, and jostling, and loathsome sights and abominable smells. Clamorous beggars, wretched with unsightly disease, are suddenly thrust under their eyes, and accost them as "Father and Mother." They have to force their way among importunate rival shopkeepers, who crowd round their vehicles and disparage each other's goods and character.

"Madam, that fellow big rascal. He tell big lie. He nothing got. I everything got it. English ribbon, lovely as butter. I very good man." The unpaved lanes are too narrow for carriages to pass each other safely. Wheel gets locked within wheel, and the passenger has to get out and pick her way as she can.

A flight of steps leads to an upper story of passages and shops—a network of galleries in perpetual gloom. The whole seems so shaky and rotten, you can fancy it might tumble together and bury buyers, sellers, and wares in one ruin. In some of these sheds, though there is scarcely room to turn, there are very costly wares, beautiful fabrics, and jewels of immense value. The shopkeeper pulls out bundle after bundle, and discloses the most exquisite draperies a woman's eyes ever feasted on. Lovely Cashmere robes and shawls, silk gossamers embroidered in gold, delicately fine Dacca muslins, transparent fabrics woven from the fibre of the pine-apple, rarities seldom found in even the best English shops.

I gave a specimen of the English sometimes heard in the bazar. Here is a shopkeeper's advertisement I once met with.

"Messrs. Nondo Lall Paul and Co. begs to intimate that Nondo Lall Paul and Co. was opened a Bonnet Shop at —— Bazar for 2 years, and they has experienced all the time the best rich straw and silk bonnets to the Ladies for their order, and now they invites all the Ladies that whatever sorts of Bonnets given to order shall be faithfully executed with good English materials, etc. New Millinery and Straw Bonnets investment for the season they has also opened for sale at a cheap price."

I have met with two mistakes in England with regard to native acquaintance with the English language. In the first place some persons have thought that such specimens as the above represent the whole result of costly educational efforts to confer on the people of India the intellectual and moral wealth enshrined in our English literature. Such specimens would appear as ridiculous in India as they appear here. I have been struck with the perfect knowledge of English shown by Bengalis who never were away from their native land, and whose daily speech in their homes is Bengali. Many in England will remember the power and eloquence of the late Kesab Chunder Sen, the Brahmo leader, when addressing audiences in this country some years ago. I know Bengalis who, so far as idiom is concerned, would speak with equal or even greater purity. When listening to a religious address given to our students by Babu Kali Choron Bannerji, of the Free Church Mission, I have thought that a speech of the same length from Keshub Chunder Sen would not have been so perfectly free from errors of idiom, whatever surpassing qualities of feeling and fancy there might have been. The Bengali gentleman who has successfully contested an English constituency for a seat in Parliament, speaks with a clearness, directness, and purity which remind one of the late John Bright.

As to the second mistake, it seems to be thought by some that the English tongue will, in time, supersede the native languages in India. I have never met with any one acquainted with India who thought so. There are many thousands of English-speaking natives. But they are only a handful of the people. Bengali, Urdu, Hindi, in North India, will be spoken by populous nations when English shall be unknown or little known in the land. Through their own vernaculars, therefore, the masses of the people must be evangelised, and this by men of God raised up in thousands from the people, for thousands are needed.

We have always regarded our native preachers as the richest fruit of our educational work.

Jews are numerous in Calcutta, and many of them are wealthy. The most palatial mansion on the Chowringhee Road belongs to a Jew. The summer retreat at Darjeeling, among the Himalayas, which rivals that of the Lieutenant-Governor of Bengal, is the residence of a Calcutta Jew.

You see the Mussulman pause in his walk over the Maidan; he spreads a cloth on the ground, kneels with his face towards Mecca, and bows his head again and again to the ground, absorbed in evening worship. You hear a voice from some neighbouring Mosque calling "the faithful" to prayer. In one of the public squares you might see, of an evening, crowds gathered round the respective preachers of different faiths—Christian, Brahmo, Hindu, Mussulman. Let us look at the Muhammadan company. There is a crowd of onlookers standing round the outskirts. Making your way through this fringe, you see a remarkable sight: a sea of "the faithful" seated on the ground, silent, motionless. I remember such a scene. They are listening with upturned faces and rapt attention to the preacher of Islam. He is a little thin man. How impassioned and earnest he is; and how they are taking it in! I remember asking, as I drew near: "What is he putting into them? what is he feeding them with?" He closes his address, and, at a slight movement of his hand, they all rise as one man for a prayer.

The great mass of the people of Calcutta are Hindus. Yet, if a visitor were curious to see great Hindu temples in the metropolis, such as there are in South India, he could not find any. I cannot say where there is a Hindu temple in that great city. The temple at Kalighat is miles away. Hinduism is specially a domestic religion. It is in the people's homes and lives. Its hold is on their every action. It does not need the temples. In each house there is a shrine.

The only respectable heathen temple I know of in Calcutta is a Jain temple. Jainism is the Indian representative of Buddhism. In its moral teachings and ideas respecting the future, it has much in common with Buddhism. Yet the Jains have a modified belief in certain Hindu gods, as Brahma, Vishnu, Siva, and Gunes. Representations of these deities, and of indecent legends connected with them, I have sometimes seen on Jain temples. They reverence the vital principle in all living things. "Do not kill or injure." "Strict Jains carry this injunction to so preposterous an extreme that they strain water before drinking it, sweep the ground with a brush before treading on it, never eat or drink in the dark." At the temple in Calcutta, I saw several priests with muslin covers over their mouths as a security against the risk of swallowing minute insects. This scrupulous regard for life brings its inconveniences. In some parts of India people will not light a lamp after sunset. Through long hours of the night they sit in darkness in their cheerless houses, lest, if they light a lamp, insects should perish in the flame.

The Jains are known as "a wealthy community, usually engaged in banking or wholesale commerce, and of boundless charity."

To a stranger moving about the streets and bazars

of native Calcutta, it might seem that the place is wholly heathen, and that Christianity has made little or no impression: the multitude of Hindus is so vast, and the indications of heathenism are everywhere noticeable. But further observation would be a corrective to such an impression.

I have not yet referred to the Christian aspects and the Christian community, of Calcutta. The lofty flat roof of our institution in the southern suburb commands a wide view of the city and neighbourhood. From that position so many spires of Christian churches can be seen that one might think he was looking over a Christian city. I have stood there and counted nine or ten church steeples, and they are not the whole of the Christian sanctuaries. The spired churches are Episcopalian, Presbyterian, and Roman Catholic. There are also at least six sanctuaries belonging to Methodists, Baptists, and Congregationalists. In all these English and Eurasian Christians meet for worship. There are hundreds of godly men and women in these congregations who desire that the light of the Gospel may be diffused throughout India, and who seek the good of the land in which Providence has cast their lot. There are devout English women, mothers in Israel, who feel a kindly concern for young men from England's homes, and whose houses are open to give them welcome in that land of exile and heathenism. Their own children away in England by a sad necessity, they comfort their motherly hearts, and serve their Lord, by showing kindness to the sons of far-off mothers.

Still further there are at least ten places of worship

for native Christian congregations connected with the various missions. Thus, without giving exact statistics, I have indicated twenty-six Christian churches, larger or smaller, European and native, which are, more or less, centres of light in that great heathen city and country.

CHAPTER XIV.

NOT LONG AGO.

STATUES in memory of distinguished men are numerous in Calcutta. Few linger to notice them in an atmosphere of fire. In front of one of the public buildings, yet partly hidden in the shade of trees, there is a monument I have looked on with deep interest. Around the circular pedestal there are carved figures representing a Suttee. The body of the husband lies on the pile. There is a figure holding a flaming torch. The young widow about to ascend the pile has just made over her babe to a man standing near. She has turned to her child for a last look, and the little one is stretching out its arms to her. Above is the statue of Lord Bentinck. On the pedestal is an inscription written by Macaulay, which summarises that nobleman's excellencies and the beneficial results of his government. It runs thus :—

"This statue is erected to Lord William Cavendish Bentinck, who, during seven years, ruled India with eminent prudence, integrity, and benevolence ; who, placed at the head of a great empire, never laid aside the simplicity and moderation of a private citizen ;

who infused into Oriental despotism the spirit of British freedom; who never forgot that the end of government is the welfare of the governed; who allowed liberty to the expression of public opinion; whose constant study it was to elevate the moral and intellectual character of the government committed to his charge; this monument was erected by men who, differing from each other in race, in manners, and in religion, cherish, with equal veneration and gratitude, the memory of his wise, upright, and paternal administration."

One of his most famous and humane measures was the abolition of Suttee throughout India in 1829. So far into the present century, and within the memories of men now living, was this inhuman rite practised. This and other inhumanities that have ceased do not belong to a remote past. They lie only a few years behind us. In my early days, an old citizen of Calcutta said to me: "When I think of what India was forty years ago, and what it is to-day, I am amazed at the change." There were men who declared that the abolition of the Suttee would be attended with the highest degree of danger; some opposed such interference with the customs of the people, and asserted their right to do as their forefathers had done for generations. Wonderful it seems with what ease the reform was accomplished. Many governors had shrunk from it with apprehension. The Act was passed, and the horrible rite dropped out of existence. Ten years after my arrival in Calcutta, a brother missionary addressed an audience on his missionary reminiscences. He was an old man, and his "recollections" were listened to with intense interest.

In his early days he was present at a Suttee. "I can never forget it," he said. "It was about 5 p.m. when I arrived. The crowd was very great. In the centre was a pile of wood. The corpse of the husband lay upon it. On the north side of it was a palanquin containing the young widow to be immolated. Brahmans stood around. I got permission to speak to her; but on attempting to do so, I found her so under the influence of drugs as to render the effort useless. The Brahmans made short work of it. On my leaving the palanquin they took her out of it, and endeavoured to lead her round the pile, but she was unable to stand. She was taken up and carried round it once only (they ought to have gone round it seven times), when they laid the poor creature upon her wooden bed beside the corpse of her husband. At this moment she seemed conscious of what was before her, for she instantly threw her arms around its neck and embraced the corpse with great affection. The Brahmans, however, lost no time in finishing their dreadful work. Immediately they began to heap upon the bodies the remainder of the pile, until they covered them at least two feet—a weight of wood sufficient to crush the very bones themselves; and to make all the more sure, they bound down the whole pile with bamboos crossed over, lest the poor victim, in her struggles on feeling the fire, should toss it off and escape. All being duly secured, a boy of about twelve years of age, probably the brother of the widow, came forward with a lighted torch and set fire to the pile close to the head of the victim. At this moment gongs and drums struck up their deafening sounds, while the vast multitude of spectators joined in shouts of 'Hori Bole, Hori Bole,' thus effectually drowning the shrieks of the poor dying creature. This was a scene enough at the time to freeze the warmest love a missionary might have brought to the Hindu nation."

"To obtain an idea of the native mind generally, it should be borne in mind that when help did come, it was not in the least from the native world; not a finger did it raise, not a sign did it make, but that of complaisance in these national murders—nay, to the eternal disgrace of native Calcutta, in 1834, 18,000 persons, many of them of the highest families in the city and neighbourhood, were found to unite in a petition to the Privy Council complaining of Lord William Bentinck's suppression of Suttee, and praying for its restoration." The disgrace called "eternal" belongs to the Calcutta of 1834, not to that of 1892.

India has suffered deeply from famines. The land is not free from them yet. But they are not so frequent or so terrible as they were formerly. Referring to the great calamity of 1769-70, the historian of "Rural Bengal" declares that "the failure of a single crop, following a year of scarcity, swept away ten millions of human beings. This famine explains those broad tracts of desolation which the English conquerors found everywhere throughout the lower valley."

Coming nearer our own times, we read in the *Calcutta Chronicle*: "It is really shocking to humanity to behold, in the streets of Calcutta, so many poor wretches dying of hunger, chiefly women and children. Not an instance occurs of the least assist-

BURNING THE DEAD.

ance being afforded to any of them by their callous and inhuman countrymen." My knowledge of the conduct of native gentlemen, during a time of dearth in still more recent years, does not tally with the closing assertion in the above quotation.

Through the failure of the crops in Orissa in 1866, a million and a quarter of people perished. Multitudes from the famine-stricken districts flocked to Calcutta for food. Many died on the way. The report of the health officer of Calcutta stated that as many as ten thousand of the starving people were being fed by native gentlemen. At one of the ghats there were four thousand five hundred people to whom food was being distributed by a wealthy Muhammadan gentleman. Four thousand and eighty pounds' weight of rice and curry were daily cooked for them. Another gentleman was feeding fifteen hundred, and still another one thousand people. I saw the sons of native gentry strip themselves of their upper garments, gird their waist-cloths about their loins, and carry food to hundreds of emaciated creatures, sitting silent and patient on the ground, with "famine" stamped on their faces.

The news of such provision drew great numbers from the rural districts to the south. With the real sufferers came multitudes of professional beggars, but they were easily distinguished from the starving population. Not only hunger but disease was pouring into the city. The immediate erection of sheds and distribution of clothing became necessary, or we might expect a frightful mortality. We were in the rains. The nights were chill. The land was sodden. There were hundreds of women suckling children who had not a rag of covering. An old soldier-friend at Hastings, in charge of stores, said to me: "There are about 600 blankets lying unused in my go-downs. Write a letter to the papers, as you happen now to know they are there, and suggest a good use for them. Somebody will see it, and I shall very likely get an order to make them over for these people." I wrote a letter, and the order came from head-quarters. So, at any rate, six hundred shivering creatures were comforted.

Sad stories reached us from the country districts.

Two old men, driven by hunger from their village, moved feebly towards Midnapore in hope of obtaining food. One, struck by hunger and damp, died on the road under a tree. The other waked to find his companion dead and himself drenched with rain, and unable to move. The dogs and jackals began at the corpse. The living skeleton sat by, powerless to prevent them. He appealed faintly to passers-by. A European alighted from his palkee and gave the man such as he had—a little beer. It revived him, and he faltered out his tale of woe. The Englishman went away for food. On his return the man was in a state of coma, and soon died.

A dead woman was found with a living child at her breast. The stiff, cold arm had to be forced back to release the child.

A European woman asked one of our missionaries to baptise a native child which she had begged from its mother. She had said to the mother, who came to the house asking alms: "Give me your child, and I'll relieve you." The poor mother refused, and went away. The next day she came back and said:

"Take my child. I shall die. Why should the child die too?"

A gentleman who was deputed to a tour of inspection, reported that in four villages there were not more than ten houses in which there were not from one to four dead bodies. In one place there were four or five hundred dead, and most of them in houses. One "head man" said that in his village, a few months before, there were seven hundred people. Of these, not more than one hundred and sixty were left.

The Collector of Cuttack reported to Government, after personal investigation, that over the whole distance of forty-two miles, from Cuttack to Taldunah, there was not a vestige of a crop, or even an attempt at cultivation!

We may confidently hope that these desolations will be no more. They need not be. A repetition of the calamities of 1866 could scarcely be now. The food of a particular district may fail; but we may expect there will be at the same time, as there has been in famine-times before, abundance elsewhere in that vast empire. It was so during the Orissa famine. When the calamity was on us, immense stores of grain were collected, but they could not be got to the starving multitudes. Ships laden with rice, from Bengal and Burmah, lay off the coast of Orissa, but could not land their cargoes. Boats were filled again and again, and again and again were swamped in the stormy surf. These experiences have left their lessons. By watchfulness, forethought, arrangement, and increased means of inland transport, it is clear the land may be shielded from the scourge that has swept away millions from time to time. Here lies work for a strong, enlightened, and humane Government. Towards this beneficent end British rule is working. From the ravages of famine the land will have rest.

Not many decades ago, large boats might be seen coming down the river to Calcutta, filled with children for open sale as slaves. Most of them had been stolen from their parents, or bought for a measure of rice in a time of scarcity. Threepence was the price at which many a child was bought. Sir William Jones, referring to this in a charge to the grand jury in Calcutta, said : " I am assured that the condition of slaves within our jurisdiction is beyond imagination deplorable ; and that cruelties are daily practised on them, chiefly on those of the tenderest age and the weaker sex, which, if it would not give me pain to repeat and you to hear, yet, for the honour of human nature, I should forbear to particularise." Poor children ! Miserable was their lot in life ! They are comforted now. And the Spirit of Him who took the little children in His arms, put His hands on them, and blessed them, has been at work in India to shield the helpless from these inhumanities.

In the following forcible and impressive passage, a missionary friend contrasts the Calcutta of the present with the city as it was at the close of the last century. " Calcutta is still the scene of much gross immorality, of great ungodliness, and of widespread unbelief ; and its vast population of Hindus and Mussulmans is still far from the acknowledgment of the truth of the Gospel. The heart of the Christian philanthropist must sink within him as he surveys the evil which the great metropolis of India exhibits even now. Yet who can contrast the Calcutta of the present—its numerous places of worship of all denominations well filled with attentive hearers of the Gospel, its many churches of faithful men, its evangelical agencies, and its increasing community of native converts—with the city of which we have been speaking, without acknowledging that a great and happy change has been effected? We have much in our day over which to lament; but, nevertheless, 'the Lord hath done great things for us, whereof we are glad.'"

CHAPTER XV.

CHURCHES ON THE RICE-FIELDS.

THE village of Karapukur stands on the northern edge of a great rice district. It is the chief station of our rural churches in the south, and is about six miles from Calcutta. For months of the year the country is under water, and looks like a vast lake. Afterwards it is all green with the growing rice, then yellow with the ripe grain. One gets from village to village by means of boats for a good part of the year. I sometimes took the young missionary collectors of our English congregation for a day's trip to these villages. Some older Christian friends were glad to go with us. We went in carriages to Karapukur; then we took to country-boats, long, narrow, and flat-bottomed, each shaped from a single trunk. The excursion was in the cold season, but even then we had to screen ourselves from the hot sun by covering the boats with low, portable roofs of rushes, sloping down to the edge of the craft. We sat crowded, and crouching on mats, cushions, and chairs with amputated legs, in the bottom of the boat. It was an uncomfortable, cramping position. There was plenty of fresh air and plenty of nature, but they were outside with the sun. Where was the pleasure? It was a change in the weary monotony of Anglo-Indian life. There is little variety and much confinement in the lives of English and Eurasian children in India. They are

NATIVE BAZAR.

shut up most of the day because of the heat, and they see little of other scenes than those about their home. To travel in boats to the villages was a grand treat. They were excited by the unusualness of the situation. It was a break in the monotony of life.

It must not be supposed that, on their arrival, they found the village a scene of rural loveliness. There were no fields decked with daisies and buttercups; no pretty cottages with flowers and well-kept gardens; no comfortable and substantial farmhouses. Only a cluster of thatched huts with watery fields all round. I never saw a garden-plot or flowers about the home of a Bengali peasant. But the young people enjoyed the day. A good part of it was spent in the chapel for the sake of the shade. It was a pleasure to unpack the hamper, lay out the refreshments, and finally eat them. The native women came with their dark wondering babies and talked to the ladies. The men came and spoke with the Padri Sahib.

The return journey in the evening was a real pleasure. By this time the air was cool. The roofs were lifted clean off the boats. It was pleasant to hear the swish made by the boat as it cut its way through the tall rice. Then we crossed a pond, or came on wide water-ways between the rice-fields. Beautiful lotus flowers, white and rose-coloured, floated on the surface of the water. We let our hands hang in the cooling element as we glided along. All the land was silent but for our voices in talk, laughter, or hymn. We had the world to ourselves for a time, and liked it. The young people deserved the treat. They collected from seventy to ninety pounds a year for our missionary work.

A Calcutta gentleman connected with the Established Church of Scotland gives an interesting account of a visit he paid to these churches. He was thinking of Sunday schools in Scotland, and desired to interest the scholars in missionary work. He died a few years ago, one of the many Europeans who in early life succumb to the deadly climate of Bengal. He writes :—

"We wish to tell you of a very pleasant expedition we made into the country two Sundays ago, which we think would be of interest to some of your Sabbath school scholars. We had heard of the South Villages, one of the mission stations of the London Missionary Society, situated about seven miles from Calcutta, and made up our minds to pay it a visit. Miss Daniell, a Bengali friend of ours, wrote to the minister, and told him we would come and see him and his flock on the following Sunday. The minister had at one time been a high-caste Brahman, but is now an earnest and zealous preacher of the Gospel, and has jurisdiction over seven churches within a radius of thirty miles, I think he said. The total congregation of the seven churches is between 1,000 and 1,500; but the only one we have seen so far is his own, numbering nearly 300. And of it we have now to write.

"We left Calcutta about noon, and after driving out of the town, we passed along the bank of a canal, which was crowded with quaint-looking craft of all kinds, from the bhur, which resembles a large thatched hut built on a broad boat, to trunks of trees hollowed out, which come up from the Soonderbunds laden with rice to be sold in Calcutta.

"We passed close to clumps of palm trees, with huts of various dimensions built under their shelter. Then we passed through an expanse of rice-fields, mostly of rich yellow, ripe for the harvest; then again through groves of palm, mango, and tamarind trees, till about a quarter to two we reached our destination.

"Service commenced at two, and, till it was time to go to church, we had some conversation with the minister. The bell now began to ring, and at two o'clock we walked over to the church. Outside a bell

A PEASANT WOMAN.

was hung between two palm trees, about five feet from the ground, and a little black boy sounded the chimes with a piece of bamboo. The church we found to be pretty large in size, accommodating over 300 people.

The sides and roof were of bamboos matted and thatched, the pillars being trunks of palm trees. The congregation, who were all of the peasant, fisherman, or artisan class, were most attentive listeners. The service was in Bengali. None of them know a word of English, and, though only a few miles out of Calcutta, seldom see a European. The men sat in the middle of the building, while the women and children were seated on one side, and round the pulpit. They sang very lustily, especially the younger members of the congregation, and we were astonished to find them accompanied by a tom-tom—a species of native drum—and a pair of cymbals. The service was conducted much in the same way as in our Presbyterian churches, singing psalms and hymns, reading from the Old and New Testaments, prayer and a sermon, through all of which the interest never seemed to flag. The collection was taken in a basket and a silver plate. In the basket are put rice, eggs, fruit, etc., which are sold for the support of their catechist. In the silver plate they collect money for the same purpose. My wife went into some of the houses to see the women, who were greatly pleased at her visit. The country all around looked very pretty, like a Sunday at home in the country, everything was so calm and peaceful. We spent a very pleasant day, and were greatly interested in hearing the history of the South Village Mission." This gentleman and his wife were much interested in our Village Mission. At the invitation of the native pastor, they paid a second visit, and were present at the annual gathering of the seven churches on the New Year's Day, 1888. Of this visit Mrs. Cruden wrote :—

"New Year's Day, so suggestive of frost and snow and blazing fires, has no such associations to us here in the City of Palaces. This morning the air is just cold enough to be pleasant, the sky a deep cloudless blue, and the sun shining brilliantly, as it has been doing for the last two months, and which we can count on its doing steadily for some months to come, which is more than one can do in the old country.

"After breakfast, accompanied by friends, making in all a party of eight, we started for our seven miles' drive. About 11.30 we arrived at the pretty little thatched church, to find that the service had already begun; so we slipped in quietly,—not an easy matter, as the church was very crowded.

"It is a picturesque gathering. White is the prevailing colour, and very snowy white it is too, lit up here and there by the brilliant red or green saris of the women. Occasionally the little children get restless, and have to be carried out and soothed by their sweet-faced dark mothers; but the large congregation is wonderfully quiet, and we are struck by the look of interested attention specially on the faces of the men.

"How we wish some of our friends from home could be with us to-day! The sight of this large congregation of native Christians, coming from villages scattered over the rice-fields, would rejoice their hearts, and encourage them to renewed efforts to send more light to these dark lands.

"There are others too that we could wish were here, those who are asking: 'What good are missions doing?' We would like to point them to the hundreds here to-day, and tell them that this is the result of a few words spoken many years ago by a missionary to the forefathers of some of these very men."

The event which stands at the beginning of this good work is graphically described by Dr. Mullens in his Memorials of Mr. Lacroix. Near the bank of a water-way which runs southward into the great rice

RICE-BOATS.

district stands the busy market of Chitla, much frequented by the people of the South Villages for the sale of their grain and fish. The missionaries of the London Missionary Society were accustomed to preach in a shed they had built near this market, on the bank of the canal. "One day early in 1825, Mr. Trawin was preaching to a large congregation drawn around him from the market, when he was rudely interrupted by a sturdy-looking farmer, who angrily demanded why he spoke against their religion. Mr.

Trawin calmly replied that he was endeavouring, for their benefit, to exhibit the true way of salvation. A brief discussion ensued on the relative merits of Hinduism and Christianity; and the farmer and his companions were invited by Mr. Trawin to visit him at his own house. The little party came again and again, especially on the Sabbath-days; the nature, views, doctrines, moral precepts, fruits and hopes of the Gospel were expounded clearly, and contrasted with the deep defects and vital errors of Hindu idolatry; and the result was a growing conviction upon their minds that the former religion was true. These discussions were reported to their neighbours and friends, among whom Christianity in all its aspects was a perfectly new and unknown thing.

"The inquirers were all men in the prime of life, of sober character and sound sense. They were also men of substantial means, having lands, houses, farms, boats, and fishing grounds. Ramji Pramanik, the principal inquirer, was deeply impressed by the Gospel. He had been for years seeking something which should satisfy those longings of his soul which Hinduism could not reach. He drank in the truth with a sincere heart, and in him it brought forth fruit abundantly. His two friends were equally honest and sincere; and at length, on the 18th of October 1825, they were baptised. As many of their friends seemed anxious to learn about this new doctrine, Mr. Trawin frequently went among them in order to expound the way of God more perfectly. A small cottage, used as a place of worship, was soon found to be too small. Men and women gathered in large numbers on the Sabbath; and a school was opened, which soon numbered sixty boys. It was resolved, therefore, to erect a large chapel, and provide accommodation for the occasional visits of the missionary. The village in which these pleasant occurrences were taking place is called Rammakalchoke ; it is situated eight miles south of Calcutta. Ramji was the largest landholder in the place, and resolved to help the project of a new chapel in an unusual way. On one portion of his land stood a small temple of Siva ; it was a kind of family temple, and the Brahman in charge received more support from the family than from any one else. As it was his own property, Ramji resolved to pull it down and give its materials for a place of Christian worship. This required considerable courage, which, however, he was enabled to put forth. On a certain day, in the presence of a great crowd who manifested much excitement, Ramji brought out the idol, and flung it on the ground. The Brahman exclaimed in horror, almost in the language of Micah : 'Ye have taken away my god, and what have I more?' The temple soon disappeared, and the new chapel rose in its place, with a bungalow on the roof for the missionary's residence. The whole was completed and set apart for worship on the 7th of November, 1826. The opening sermons were preached to crowded congregations. The idol was forwarded to the Society in England."

Mr. Trawin's name is not on that sad list I have copied from the tablet in Union Chapel. He came to Calcutta in 1819. He learnt the vernacular quickly and well, and gave himself to preaching the Gospel in Bengali. He itinerated frequently from village to village, and found great acceptance among the

Hindus, to many of whom his preaching was greatly blessed. The great movement of inquiry and conversion in the south country at that time, by which hundreds were brought from darkness to the light of the Gospel, was primarily owing to his labours. He died far from the scene of his useful and happy work. In 1828 he took his little daughter a river trip to Berhampur, on account of her health. There she died; and her father lived but a few days after her, passing away at the early age of thirty-two, after nine years of missionary work. The distinguished itinerating preacher, Mr. Lacroix, took his first itinerancy in Mr. Trawin's company, "and to the last days of his life never uttered his name, or described his useful labours, except in terms of warm admiration, respect, and love."

CHAPTER XVI.

A PEERESS AMONG THE PEASANTS.

THE village of Karapukur was once honoured by the presence of Lady Dufferin. The visit was merely a call by the way. There she was to take the little canoe waiting to convey her along the unwholesome ditches which traverse the rice-fields. She was on her way to one of the stations of the S.P.G., which lies further in the heart of these dreary marshes. The visit was thus an accidental honour to these poor people of our London Mission, whose work does not receive much attention from the titled of the earth. The native pastor, however, properly determined to show a grateful appreciation of the interest her ladyship felt in the "poor Christians of these swampy regions." They erected what they were pleased to call "a triumphal arch" at the entrance of the village, and another near the pastor's house, bearing the inscription, "Welcome." These "triumphal arches" consisted of bamboos, leaves, and a few wild flowers, and, in accordance with the circumstances of the people, cost some three or four shillings the pair. The reader must not, therefore, picture to himself anything like the "Arc de Triomphe" in Paris. They were put up, however, by willing hands, and with hearts whose feeling was—

> "We give thee all, we can no more,
> Though poor our offering be."

A *shamiana*, or awning, was put up on the bank of the muddy water. Below lay the boat prepared to receive her ladyship. A cloth was spread on the ground, and a chair placed for her. The road on each side was lined with some hundreds of our native Christians, and the children of our village schools. At ten o'clock the Viceregal carriage drove up, followed by a number of the Viceroy's native body-guard. These truly tall gentlemen, on their fine chargers, and in their gorgeous coats of scarlet embroidered with gold, must have impressed the villagers very much. The Lord Bishop of Calcutta was in attendance too, and the magistrate of the district, and one or two A.D.C.'s. Now came the really interesting part of the visit. Her ladyship sat down on the solitary chair under the awning. Behind her, but at a considerable distance, at one corner of the carpet, stood an A.D.C. Her dress was simple and plain, unadorned except by the grace of the wearer. Her bearing was natural, sweet, and womanly, the kind of bearing in a woman that appeals to the hearts of the sterner sex. Our native pastor was permitted to speak to her, and read the following brief address:—

"May it please your Ladyship, we, the Christian inhabitants of the village of Karapukur, in connection with the London Missionary Society, take this occasion of your ladyship's passing through our village, to express our heartfelt pleasure and thankfulness to you for the interest your ladyship has taken in the Christian inhabitants of this country.

"The fatiguing journey your ladyship has undertaken to visit the poor Christians of these swampy regions, is itself a great proof of your interest in them. Poor as we are, we could scarcely expect a visit from a person of so exalted a position. This is the first instance of such an act of kindly interest and condescension on the part of the consort of the Viceroy and Governor-General. And though the visit is not to our own station, the pleasure to us is all the same.

"May our common Lord and Saviour bless your ladyship, and the noble Earl, our Governor-General, and the other members of your family, for the kindness you have shown to your poor Christian brethren and sisters in these regions!

"Signed on behalf of the Christians of the London Missionary Society in these parts, by

"TIN KAORI CHATERJI, *Pastor.*

"*February 24th,* 1887."

Her ladyship went up to the pastor and spoke kindly to him. She said: "It's very kind of you, I'm sure, to take all this trouble," expressed her good wishes for him and his work, and shook hands with him.

She then went down the bank into the boat. A light covering made of rushes, and resembling an elongated extinguisher, was put on the boat to screen her from the fierce rays of the sun.

The party, viceregal, episcopal, and civil, then passed on towards the place they were bound for, leaving Karapukur, after this brief burst of glory, to its normal quiet and obscurity. The great have to leave pomp behind them when they proceed onward from the village to the rice-fields and marshes further south. There are no roads for carriages and horses. The coats of scarlet and gold, together with their wearers, and the steeds, rested, therefore, under the pleasant shade of trees while their mistress went forward on her fatiguing and somewhat perilous journey. I say perilous, for the season was too far advanced for such a journey. The heat was intense. The odour from the dirty water and muddy banks was offensive and unwholesome. Many a one of us followed the brave countess with the wish that no evil in the shape of malarial fever might touch her. The district is the home of fever and cholera. It was a journey which few English ladies in India would have cared to face in that season. We heard that her ladyship went into several of the poor people's huts. Doubtless her kindly spirit would be touched by the cheerless condition in which millions of human beings over whom her husband ruled were destined to pass their lives. Indeed, as abodes of God's children in this world, there appears too sad a contrast between the palace of a Viceroy and the hut of a very poor Bengali peasant. But the pastor, with truth and modesty, could speak to the peeress of "our common Lord and Saviour."

Our Christians of the south villages live in out-of-the-way places. Their congregations are scattered far and wide over these rice-lands. They are very poor, many of them are unspiritual and quite uneducated. "Yet, I must say," their pastor remarked on a late occasion, "that there are some, and their number is not small, with whom to talk is to enjoy heaven on earth, and you cannot but love them and long for their company."

CHAPTER XVII.

THE OLD MUSSULMAN CAPITAL AND ITS PROVINCE.

I TOOK the train at Calcutta one afternoon to visit our Murshedabad Mission, and reached Nulhati on the East Indian Railway about eleven o'clock. There I passed an uneasy night on the table of the waiting-room. At 4 a.m. I was called to get a train by another line, a "State Railway," which runs eastward for twenty-five or thirty miles to the populous town of Azimgunge on the "sacred" Bhagaruttee. I have no pleasant recollections of that journey. The sight of the dreary plain between Nulhati and Azimgunge recalled to my mind Milton's description of another plain, "forlorn and wild, the seat of desolation." Then, four or five hours for some twenty-five miles give too large an opportunity for contemplating such scenery. And to get relief from the intolerable jolting of the train, I had to stand on a little platform at the end of the carriage and cling with both hands to an iron rail to steady myself. Things are better now.

At Azimgunge a brother missionary, the Rev. W. B. Phillips of Berhampur, met me. He had brought his little missionary boat, the *Jessie.* Breakfast was soon ready in the neat, tiny cabin. We were to drop down the river to Berhampur. It was still early morning. How delightful it was, after a restless night, to lie on the bunk and feel the fresh morning air through the open windows! How pleasant was the smooth, noiseless motion! How beautiful the gleam and sparkle of the waters in the morning sun! We passed the great deserted palace of the Nawab of Murshedabad, and saw some of the old barges in which royal parties—the women of the harem especially—used to take their pleasure. In these painted and gilded boats they floated along to the sound of music and song. A few hours brought us to the centre of our missionary work in the district, Berhampur.

The words of Christ apply emphatically to the district of Murshedabad: "The harvest truly is plenteous, but the labourers are few." Many years ago, the Bengal census reported a population of more than one million three hundred thousand in the district. Among this great population—about equal to half the number of people in Lancashire—we have had for years at a stretch only one European male missionary, at other times two. For some months there were three. The number had dropped again to one in 1892, but has since been raised to three. The London Mission is the only one in the district.

The visitor to Berhampur in these days is struck with the silence and emptiness of the place. Two generations ago it showed a very different sight. Then, it was a great military station. The noble and extensive barracks built by Lord Clive, and said to be the finest in India, were filled with English soldiers. The vast grassy square, skirted on three sides by these buildings, and open towards the river, was alive at daybreak with troops on parade. In the evening, on the broad promenade along the bank of the river, English ladies and gentlemen in carriages, on horseback, on foot, enjoyed the cool air, while military bands played sweet music. There were large silk factories in the neighbourhood. The English chapel was filled, week after week, with soldiers and civilians, to many of whom the earnest ministrations of Mr. Micaiah Hill, the founder of the mission, were greatly blessed. Now the barracks are silent and empty. The great square is deserted. The promenade is no longer a scene of life and gaiety. The large public gardens, when I saw them, were lapsing into a tangled wilderness. The serpentine lake, once a pleasant rowing ground, was choked with reeds and rushes, and showed a ruined boat-house and a leaky boat. The reason for this standing camp, and for the change, is not far to seek. A few miles distant along the river is the Muhammadan city of Murshedabad, the old capital and court of the ruler of Bengal, a place and power once hostile to the British rule. The city had to be overawed, and troops kept in readiness for exigencies. It was a Nawab of Murshedabad who perpetrated the horrors of the Black Hole in Calcutta. The Nawab is no longer formidable to the British Government. His power to harm is gone. His great palace is not used, except on rare state occasions, or as a sight to the traveller who can turn aside to see out-of-the-way places. Murshedabad has sunk into insignificance and decay.

It appears to the passing traveller as little more than a palace, the ruins of a few mansions, and a collection of miserable huts. The population, however, is still large. As to Berhampur, though its glory as a military station and the scene of a busy European life, has passed away, the importance of the place as a centre for missionary operations among a large population has not diminished.

The mission was commenced in 1824 by the Rev. Micaiah Hill. In January, 1891, there died at Berhampur an old missionary who will be long and affectionately remembered in the district—Samuel John Hill. He was the son of the founder of the mission, and himself for long years a devoted labourer there. He was a man with rare qualifications for his work, and of singular devotedness. At the time of his death, twenty-seven years had passed without a visit to England. So long a stay in the exhausting climate of Bengal, without the change which for an Englishman is necessary to prevent the entire collapse of health, did undoubtedly enfeeble his constitution, and probably shortened his life. He lived, however, for sixty-five years, and of these years about fifty-six were spent on the burning plains and malarious marshes of Lower Bengal.

Mr. Hill was born at Berhampur, and there, as I have said, he died. There is something pathetic and beautiful in the fact that on the same spot where the old missionary closed his eyes on the world, his mother, sixty-five years before, prayed over her new-born babe, and consecrated him to the Lord, asking that he might be a missionary somewhere in the Master's broad fields of service. How encouraging to faith and prayer is such an instance! It is a sweet and hallowing reminder of hidden spiritual forces that are within our reach—a reminder before which the doubting and uneasy spirit may be hushed into comfort, and cheered with hope. That Hindus should beg to be allowed to carry the remains of the Christian missionary to the grave was a striking and appropriate tribute of esteem for one who had sacrificed fortune and worldly position, and spent his life for the good of the people of the land. Our brother Hill had done all this.

Berhampur is the one centre of light for the million and half of the Murshedabad district. The mission boat, built and used for years by Mr. Phillips, goes up and down the river, visiting the towns and villages on and near the banks. The position of the river favours this work. It runs due south, and bisects the district into two nearly equal portions. The starting of an Anglo-Vernacular Mission School by Mr. Hill gave new life to the Berhampur Mission. It brought the missionary into close contact with many young men. He formed Bible Classes which he taught in his own home. The seed of the Word was sown in many hearts. Some have made confession unto salvation, and are serving the Lord in teaching, in preaching, in civil employ under Government. The present superintendent of the Mission School, Babu Kali Prosonno Mukerji, M.A., is a convert from the school.

In a quiet lane there is a chapel called "The Magazine," a singular name for a Christian sanctuary. Its walls and roof are of immense strength. In the old military days it was a storehouse for gunpowder.

The name is retained: the use is changed. I have often in that quiet sanctuary enjoyed the privilege of Christian worship with Hindu fellow-believers.

Light and comfort are reaching the women in villages and Zenanas. "Berhampur," writes a Christian worker, "presents a very large field in itself, and there are many villages lying on the outskirts which I long to visit. Our work lies chiefly among the poor. The houses generally are small, only a mud-hut, with one small room, and a thatched verandah. In many of these we have sat and talked; also by the roadside, under the shade of trees, wherever the people could be found. We have gone to distant villages, have crossed the river by ferry-boats, always to find a welcome. Many a mother, mourning over the death of her child, has been soothed, and the story of Jesus' love has become in many homes a familiar story."

On the other hand, caste and prejudice often make it difficult to gain entrance into houses. Sometimes arrangements are made for regular lessons, "but after only a few visits of real enjoyment, because of the interest shown, suddenly a fear spreads among the women, and an excuse is made to discontinue their lessons."

The Bible work and Zenana visitation are being rapidly extended. There are encouragements and cheering incidents. In some quarters "open doors are numerous, and opportunities of work far beyond our power. Hardly a week has passed without an invitation to some new house."

In some Zenanas the women "always have a hearty greeting for us, and the Gospel message seems to be welcome to them. A mother said to the Christian teacher: 'I have been hoping every day you would come soon; all the children are ill, and I am in great trouble; but if I hear your words, my mind will feel happier.' A Babu stopped one of our teachers, and told her his wife was very sad and always crying, for she could not get over the trouble of parting with her two little girls, who had recently been married. But she had said she thought she should be happy again if she might learn from us." Cruelly does Hinduism bear on loving mothers and their little girls; but the Redresser of wrongs and Healer of sorrows has entered the land. "In Him shall these sad souls find peace."

There is a little grave I wished to see during my visit to Berhampur. It is in a disused cemetery for Europeans, a neglected, melancholy spot. My missionary brother Hill undertook to guide me to it. We climbed a wall, picked our way along grass-grown paths, and stepped over graves partly hidden by the luxuriant vegetation. For a time my companion seemed not sure of the exact spot. He searched about, and pushed aside the long seed-grass with his stick. At last he pointed to a mound and said: "That is the grave."

There is a peculiar sadness in a visit to those silent enclosures in India which are consecrated to English dead. In the epitaphs there are echoes from far-off English homes, from villages and towns whose names are familiar to us. The occupants, marching with the ever-changing English hosts that pass over the land, have here dropped by the way. They seem so entirely forgotten. Their resting-place is seldom visited. In this old cemetery are the ashes of military officers, and civil servants, and ladies who once had sway in the bright days of the station. My visit was to the resting-place of a child of eight years.

Years ago, natives at Cawnpore, in the North-west Provinces, used to point out a house once occupied by an English lady, Mrs. Sherwood. Mrs. Sherwood was the writer of a beautiful little story, formerly well known to young people in England, "Little Henry and his Bearer." In addition to beauty of style, and an affecting narrative, it contains, so far as it goes, a true representation of Anglo-Indian life. The poor child, so runs the story, was left an orphan before he was a year old, and for years the love of his heathen servant was all the human love he knew.

A copy of this story came into the hands of a little boy in the United States. He read it with tears, and resolved that when he grew up he would be a missionary in India. I received a call one day in Calcutta from a gentleman who had come from America for missionary work. This was he whose heart, in his boyhood, had been touched by the story of "Little Henry." He was on his way to Cawnpore, where the writer of the book had lived. In that city of tragic memories connected with the Mutiny, he took an important part in the opening services of a new large church. Many hundreds filled the church on the occasion, and about the doors there was as large a number who could not gain admission.

It was the grave of little Henry to which my friend pointed when he said: "That is the grave."

"Out of the mouth of babes and sucklings hast Thou ordained strength."

CHAPTER XVIII.

ABOUT THE PEASANTRY ON PLAIN AND HILL.

BENGALI Zemindars have often bitterly opposed the introduction of the Christian religion among their tenantry.

Many years ago Christianity found its way into a certain village of Bengal. The Hindu landlord was determined that the hated religion should not take root on his estate. He took steps to harry his Christian tenants from their lands. He found pretexts to vex them, seized many of them, carried them off to distant places, and kept them in confinement for weeks, so that their friends could not know where they were. He levelled their cottages to the ground, and removed the materials. Their goods were appropriated by men whom he had brought from a distance, to help in the work of destruction. The converts were a poor and ignorant people, but in one cottage at least there was an entire copy of the Scriptures. This came into the possession of one of the spoilers, who took it home, and whenever his children wanted paper for a kite, or some other toy, he tore a few leaves out of the book. One day a young man from a neighbouring village, a carpenter, visited the house. He also was a heathen man, but with some desire for knowledge. Seeing this large book going to destruction, he begged it, took it to his house, and began to read it in private with his father. They read together for months, and the light of truth shined into their hearts. They believed. The old man at last thought it was time to take a decided step. He invited one day a number of Brahmans to his house, and they sat far into the night discussing Christianity and Hinduism. At length the old man said to his visitors: "Well, I have listened to your arguments, and they have only served to convince me more firmly that the book is right and you are wrong. From this time I have done with Hinduism for ever." There is an interesting sequel to this story. In course of time the book, read and re-read, worn, torn, and incomplete, was sent to Calcutta to the Baptist Mission press to be rebound. The owners feared that Christian friends in the city might wish to present them with a new book instead of patching up the old one. With the Bible came this message: "We wish to have our own book returned. No other could ever be the same to us."

The admission of a Bengali peasant to church membership is sometimes a very simple matter. A missionary went into the country to see a number of villagers who desired to be received into church fellowship. He was to question them on their ideas of religious truth, their acquaintance with Scripture, and their spiritual experiences, and so judge of their fitness for membership. Now to come before the European missionary to be examined was a very formidable thing to these simple-minded peasants. One of them was specially timid. He was afraid he should not be found worthy when his turn came. He could not stand an examination. I can imagine him putting his hands together, as they do, in a supplicating manner, as he said :—

PEASANT WOMAN AND CHILD.

"Sahib, I shall never be able to answer questions. Please don't examine me."

The missionary saw the man's trepidation, and that questions would only confuse him.

"Well, what's to be done?" said he.

"If you would ask me to pray, Sahib, I think I could do that."

"Very good," said the missionary, "you shall pray. Brethren, let us pray!"

The company kneeled down, and the man, so timid before his fellow-man, poured out freely to his Maker a prayer so earnest, so devout, so evangelical, so lofty in its spiritual aspirations, that there was no more question of examining him. He "passed with honours," and was received into Christian fellowship.

A few years ago the pastor of the village churches furnished me with a fact which, as he said, "shows what the people think of us and our religion." It marks the growing influence of Christianity among the Hindu community.

"In a village about six miles from Karapukur there were two factions, headed by two of the most influential Hindus of the place. A quarrel had arisen between them about a road which one party asserted they had the right of using for public purposes, while the other party opposed them with all their might. This contention led to lawsuits, in which each side wasted an enormous amount of money. At last the Zemindar interfered, and advised them to settle the matter by arbitration. But a difficulty was felt about the selection of arbiters in whom both parties could place confidence. After some consultation and delay, thinking me to be a man whom neither side could corrupt, they agreed to ask me to settle their dispute. At the request of the Zemindar, I went to the village twice, and, after hearing both sides, I gave my decision, which, I am glad to say, put an end to the long-standing quarrel. The people have their own priest living not very far from their village, yet they could not depend on him, but asked a Christian missionary to help them to settle the matter."

Missionaries who have itinerated in the rural districts know the eagerness of natives to get books, and take with them a good supply of tracts and Scriptures. The distribution of these used to be a difficult business. Many of the people simply wished to get something for nothing. The paper would be useful; they didn't care for the matter printed on it. On one occasion a crowd pressed me closely, and some attempted to pull the books from me. I put my hand behind me, and said, resolutely, I would distribute no more. I was saved further trouble. Some fellow slipped behind me, and, as I spoke, whipped the whole bundle out of my hand. The people in front were mightily amused.

Missionaries now prefer to sell books rather than to give them away. There has been a scattering of the good seed on good soil. During a visit to a district of North India, a preacher sold about £20 worth of Christian publications among poor people. I have sold a large number of separate Gospels at the village market, and, early next morning, have found them in the hands of the dominie and his pupils at the village school.

I remember two curious instances of this eagerness for books. One is from the old days, the other is of recent times. Mr. Lacroix tells of a determined man who pushed his way through the crowd, and, "coming on me from behind, seized me round the waist and lifted me in his arms.

"'I want a book,' said he, 'and will not release you till I get one.'"

He must have been a sturdy fellow, for Mr. Lacroix was a tall man with a big frame and broad shoulders. He would have been a formidable antagonist with the thick stick he always carried. He called out :—

"Let me down this moment; don't you see the stick in my hand?"

"You may strike me as much as you will," the man said, "but unless I get one of your religious books, I shall not put you on the ground."

The missionary was not displeased; he promised what was asked, and was placed on *terra firma.* The man got two or three books instead of one, made a profound salam, and went away greatly delighted.

"One afternoon," writes a missionary friend, "as we were going about selling scriptures and pamphlets, a boy about twelve years of age kept begging us to let him perform some antics before us. We refused. At last, as we were standing on the bank preparing to re-embark, I noticed this boy standing on his head a few yards from us. Out of pity I threw him a pice. Great was our surprise when he jumped to his feet, picked up the coin, and offered it to the native preacher for a copy of a Gospel. We asked him if he could read. He said: No, but his elder brother could. To prove him, Mr. Chaterji gave him a Gospel and took the coin; but when we saw him going away and fingering his book with evident delight, we called him back and returned him his pice. He made his bow, and hurried off with a beaming face."

India is a land of villages rather than towns. In Bengal itinerating work is impracticable during the eight months of the year when burning heat and drenching rain prevail. But for itinerancies undertaken in the cold season, multitudes of people would seldom, if ever, hear the Gospel. The peasantry are simple, frank, and open to conviction. There are those among them who listen to the word with honest and good hearts. They read the books left with them, and believe in Jesus. "In two places we found men who confessed to their full belief in Jesus Christ. But they shrank from a public confession of faith, for fear of the persecution to which they would inevitably be exposed. I knew enough of the constitution of Hindu society to appreciate the great difficulties in their way. I could only pray the Almighty Father to watch over them, and clear the way for them."

"Has any one any questions to ask?" said a native brother, after preaching.

There was a deep silence; then a man said:—

"No, we have no questions to ask. We are like wild beasts entangled in a thicket, and we cannot find the way out. But you have come as our kind friends to show us the way."

Among the tablets in Union Chapel is one in memory of the Rev. Rudolph De Rodt. Mr. De Rodt, like Mr. Lacroix, under whose roof he lived for several years, was a native of Switzerland, and was also an itinerating missionary. For remarkable attainments in the native languages, for fervent and sterling piety, for energy and gentleness, it is recorded he had few superiors or equals in India. He died in the flower of his life, and the height of his usefulness, from the effects of a fever caught during a visit to the village churches in the south. He was only twenty-nine at the time of his death.

He delighted in itinerating labours, and made frequent tours in the provinces. I mention him here as connected, in an interesting way, with a remarkable story of missionary conquests among the hill-people in the south-west of Bengal. The mission of German brethren among the Kôls was frequently before the public in the early days of that mission. Mr. De Rodt was not a sharer in the toils and triumphs which then attracted so much attention. Yet his connection with that work was one of those vital though hidden links which we can sometimes trace in the movements of Providence.

In South-west Bengal is a hilly country, which has Orissa on the south, and Behar on the north. The hills rise to a height of from two thousand to twenty-five hundred feet above the sea, and form the broad tableland of Chota Nagpur. "Though a tableland, the surface is far from level. It presents to the eye an endless succession of undulations. On the east it looks down on the vast rice-fields of Bancoorah and Midnapur, which its many streams richly fertilise, and on the west, buried in its dense impassable jungles, lies the beautiful valley of the upper Soane." The area of the country is about equal to that of England.

Mr. De Rodt was deeply interested in the inhabitants of these hills, of whom the principal tribes are Kôls, an aboriginal people. He seems to have been the first to draw special attention to them. He itinerated in their country, and wrote a most valuable paper, a copy of which I have before me, recording his observations made on the spot.

The Kôls are an active, industrious race. They

travel all over Bengal in search of employment. Numbers of them are to be seen on the streets of Calcutta, diminutive in size, black, nearly naked, employed in mending roads and cleansing drains. The heavy oppression of rich landholders has driven many from their native soil to go forth as exiles to the Mauritius and the West Indies. In their own country great numbers of them are farm labourers, and are extremely poor. They are a light-hearted people, fond of music and dancing, and are addicted to drinking. Their religion is a form of devil-worship. They pay no homage to any beneficent Being. Their object in worship is to placate, if possible, malicious powers. Yet the idea of a good divinity had got among them. One was asked :—

"Why don't you pray to him?"

The reply was :—

"Why pray to him? He does no harm."

They are said to be remarkable for their love of truth. This quality, however, is to be found only among those who have retained their primitive habits, and have not been corrupted by intercourse with Hindus from the plains. Civil officers, whose work has brought them into daily contact with the people, have declared that a Kôl, if brought into court for some crime he has committed, will not shrink from telling the whole truth. This is illustrated by the touching confession of a man who delivered himself up for the murder of his son in the woods. The confession was taken almost verbatim from the prisoner's lips.

"Did you kill your son at Kapur?"

"Yes; I killed him."

"For what fault did you kill him?"

"He never committed any fault; we were both starving; I had nothing to give him to eat; he cried and looked in my face; he was weak, and lay down on the ground. He lay down in the jungle, and could not rise again; night was coming on, and I heard the tiger roaring, and I thought: 'He will seize you, my poor boy, if I leave you.' And so I killed him. I then buried him in a ravine, lest the wild beasts should devour him. I went away slowly, for I was weak and ill. And when I had got further into the forest, I thought I heard him call; and then I fainted away. But he calls me now every day. In the morning, and noon, and night I hear him call: 'Father, oh, father!' So I cannot eat. I cannot work. I cannot laugh. I can live no longer. So hang me, sir; kill me quick, and this wretchedness is over."

Truly, God has made of one blood all nations of men. The common heart beats strong in Englishman and Indian hill-man.

Mission work among the Kôls was commenced in 1845, nearly two years after Mr. De Rodt's death. A number of men had been sent to India by Pastor Gossner to establish a new mission in the East. Their sphere had not been fixed before leaving Germany. They were left to choose after inquiry and observation in the country. In the meantime they were residing in Calcutta with Dr. Hoeberlin.

"One morning," writes Dr. Mullens, "taking an early walk, they observed a number of natives, with dark skins, clearing the public drains, and, struck with their appearance, they asked Mrs. Hoeberlin: 'Who are these people we saw, so low and so degraded?'

She replied: 'They are Kôls from Western Bengal.' Their interest was excited, and inquiries were pushed further. In that estimable Christian lady these unexpected questions produced both wonder and delight.

COOLIE GIRL PLUCKING TEA.

She had long been deeply interested in that neglected people; she was well acquainted with the early labours among them of the late Mr. De Rodt, and with his affecting descriptions of their degradation. She therefore pressed their case upon the brethren, who were pleased with the fields opened before them."

The result was the establishment of a mission at Ranchee, the capital of the province.

Few of the younger members of the present generation are acquainted with the Pentecostal successes reported by the German brethren, which gratified the Christian public a little more than thirty years ago. I shall therefore go a little beyond the limits which, perhaps, in strictness should be observed in this brief sketch, and shall set down a few facts from the early history of that interesting mission. The missionary band numbered six. Setting to work as artisans, with their own hands they built houses for themselves—pretty German cottages, very small, not suited to India, fatally deficient in relief and protection from the severities of the climate. Incautiously they exposed themselves to burning suns and drenching rains in a tropical land, and "they paid the penalties of inexperience. Within a few years four of their number died; and one of their earliest possessions in the province was a burial-place for their Christian dead." For four years they saw no fruit of their labour. They were discouraged, and had thoughts of breaking up the mission and going down to work among the natives of the plains. They wrote to Gossner in despair: "This is a barren soil. We think we had better leave it and try elsewhere." He replied: "Go on, working and praying. Success is with God." A circumstance occurred which afforded a faint ray of promise. One day four men came and requested the missionaries to show them Jesus Christ, saying they were inclined to become Christians. Of course they went away disappointed. After a time they returned and begged to be allowed to go once to the English service. They gave no reason for this request; but they had a suspicion that the missionaries showed Jesus to Europeans at the English service, but would not show Him to natives. They received permission, and found that no difference was made in this matter between Europeans and natives. The first fruits were gathered in 1850. Eleven of the people were then baptised. There was no great measure of prosperity before the Mutiny; but year by year there was a steadily increasing number of converts, until in 1857 the native Christian community numbered 800 individuals. In that year the storm of rebellion burst over the land. "The Ramgarh battalion that held the province mutinied, and every Englishman, civil and military, of all ranks, fled for his life. Before many hours had passed every bungalow was in flames; the mission houses were stripped of their furniture and books; the church was gutted, and the organ pulled to pieces. The converts were hunted from their houses, and lost all their property; all the village chapels were unroofed and stripped, and at last, when nothing else remained, a price was set upon the converts' heads. They were compelled to hide in the jungles, and sought, though in vain, to descend the passes, which they found guarded, in order to escape to the plains. Their persecutors had seriously planned to exterminate the Christians from the province, when English troops marched up from Hazareebaugh, put an end to disorder, and captured the rebel delinquents. Their chief persecutor was hanged in the middle of Ranchee. The missionaries speedily returned; work was resumed; the congregations were regathered, and a strange measure of prosperity was henceforth granted." The spread of the work in the villages was wonderful. The people themselves did more than the missionaries. Christ was talked of and accepted in many villages which no missionary had ever visited. A missionary asked a woman who had come to Ranchee: "Who told you about Jesus Christ?" "Who?" said the woman. "Why, this teaching is all over the country." I was once speaking to one of the brethren on their successes. He said: "We have not done it. The people tell one another. Hundreds believe before we ever hear of them." In the year 1865, nine hundred and eighty-two adult persons received baptism.

A Sunday up at Ranchee is an experience not to be forgotten by a Christian visitor from the plains of Bengal, where the struggle with idolatry is so desperate. Twenty-six years ago I worshipped in the handsome church built by the German brethren. There was a congregation of about six hundred hill-people. They used to come to the Sabbath services from villages ten and twenty miles distant. Ranchee was then the only station of the mission. Central stations have since been established for groups of villages. The service was beautiful, simple, solemn. The congregation listened to the preacher with serious, wakeful attention. The sweetness of the music and singing steals into the heart and helps devotion. For this effective part of the service the children have been well trained by their German teachers. A large Gothic building was at that time in course of erection for the training of teachers and preachers for the villages.

A few years before my visit the excellent Bishop Cotton spent a Sunday at Ranchee, and at the service one hundred and forty-three persons, adults and children, were baptised. During this ceremony, which was celebrated with great solemnity in the chancel, the "Te Deum" was sung in Hindi at the west end of the church. The good bishop was deeply impressed. Being asked, as he went away from the church, what he thought of the service, he was silent for a time, and then said with quivering lip: "Sublime, the only word to describe it."

I cannot forbear a word of respect to the memory of one whose devoted life and truly Christian character deepened the impression made by his strange, sad death. One night, when Bishop Cotton was on visitation in his diocese, he was returning to his boat, which lay in the stream a few feet from the shore. His wife was in the cabin awaiting his return. He tried in the darkness to cross the bare plank, placed, without due safeguard, from the deck to the shore. Confused by the unsteady reflection of a lamp or torch which flashed and danced on the restless waters, he took a false step, fell into the river, and no trace of him, not even a garment or fragment of one, was ever found.

Statistics are generally uninteresting, but they are instructive. Returning for a moment to the Kôls, at the end of 1861 there were two thousand four hundred converts. At the end of 1871 there were nearly twenty-eight thousand. In 1881 the native Christian community numbered forty-four thousand and eighty-four.

CHAPTER XIX.

VISITORS FROM FRONTIER-LANDS.

A RESIDENT of Calcutta who wishes to study the races of India will find representatives of many of them somewhere about the city. A remarkable figure in the streets is the native of Afghanistan. From his bleak and barren mountains, fifteen hundred miles away, the Afghan comes down to the plains for the purposes of trade. Conspicuous by his great stature, his shaggy, black locks, and hooked nose—a mark, it is thought, of his Jewish origin—he strides along with resolute step and careless, swinging gait. Swathed in many folds of flapping, filthy cloth, he makes you not only see but feel his presence, and you cheerfully make way for him. How much life, besides that of the owner of the cloth, do those dirty garments enclose! Hill people commonly carry with them airs and odours other than those of their breezy mountains—once smelt, never forgotten!

In the habits of these Afghan traders "a relic of the old times of Asiatic trade has come down to our day. They spend their lives in carrying on traffic between India, Khorosan and Bokhara. They travel with strings of camels and ponies, banded in large armed caravans to protect themselves from the ever-recurring exactions on the road. Bullying, fighting, or bribing, they battle their way twice a year between Bokhara and the Indus." Arrived at the Indus, they have to deposit all their weapons with our officers, before they are permitted to continue their journey through India. Once within British territory, they are safe from molestation and plunder—a striking testimony to the peaceful power of British rule! Leaving wives, children, and camels in the Punjab, they scatter themselves by rail, boat, and steamer, all over the land. This continues throughout the cool season ; but as the hot weather approaches, they turn their steps northward, rejoin their families in the Punjab, return with them to their mountains, and soon begin preparations for the next year's peaceable and profitable invasion of India.

My own missionary work, unromantic and little varied, has been on the burning plains. I have never looked on the natural grandeur of Afghanistan—its scenes of savage sublimity, the Alpine forests crowning lofty mountains, the nests of rich vegetation lying here and there in deep valleys, those gloomy and awful defiles in which fifty years ago (1842) an entire British army perished. Afghanistan, though not a part of India, is, in history, politics and religion, vitally connected with India. How often has England watched with intensest interest events transpiring in that land! How often have English hearts been thrilled with news from those mountains! It is no wonder that we in Calcutta feel that there is something that bridges over the distance and brings us into touch with that far-off land and its people.

The Afghans are a wild, fierce race, inured to bloodshed from childhood, familiar with death, unsubmissive to law or discipline, unscrupulous in perjury, cruel in revenge. An unwritten code pervades the whole nation, guiding them both as to hospitality and retaliation. The Afghan is bound to feed and shelter any traveller who claims his hospitality, and to grant any boon sought by one who crosses his threshold and invokes its sanction. On the other hand, vengeance must be taken for every insult and injury, even though it may have to be delayed to the next generation; they will watch for years, and blood must be had for blood. In 1872 occurred one of the saddest tragedies in the history of our Indian rule. Calcutta was shocked by news of the assassination of the Governor-General, Lord Mayo, who had gone to the Andaman Islands to inspect the convict settlement at Port Blair. While walking there without guard or attendants very near to him,—for there was no thought of danger, a convict suddenly sprang on him from behind, and drove the long blade of a knife through his body. He was carried on board his steamboat, and soon expired. The assassin was an Afghan. There are strange contrasts in human life! The murderer had, in former days, served in an English family as bearer to a little boy, in which situation he was much liked for the qualities which native servants often show towards the little English children they have charge of—patience, gentleness, constant attention and devotion. But on his mind was the burden of avenging an injury once done to some member of his family. He found his opportunity, and killed the offender.

AFGHANS AT HOME.

For this crime he was sentenced to penal servitude for life. Among his own people there would have been no punishment or disgrace for such an act. Burning to be revenged, he saw in Lord Mayo's visit the opportunity of taking a signal vengeance, and was content to forfeit his life.

The Afghan love of independence is inextinguishable. The annals of the country tell us that a British officer of high position was pressing on a number of Sirdars the benefits of quiet and security under a strong government—benefits to be secured, of course, by submitting to a British Protectorate. An old chief gave a reply expressive of Afghan character and ways. "Sir," said he, "we are content with discord: we are content with alarms: we are content with blood; but we will never be content with a Master."

The appointment of Sir Louis Cavagnari, in 1879, to the post of British Resident at the Court of Cabul, is well remembered. He went bravely and with confidence, declaring, if not boasting, that within two years Afghanistan should be as peaceful as any part of British India. Yet some in Calcutta thought of him sadly as a doomed man. He was received with apparent cordiality. The Afghans can give way, and bide their time. Within two months the Residency was suddenly surrounded, and Cavagnari and his officers were murdered, after which, of course, an army of retribution was sent, under General Roberts.

In March of this year, 1893, the papers report the contents of a despatch sent by the Amir to our Viceroy. The Amir states that "no cause exists for British interference in his affairs. He regrets his inability to meet Lord Roberts at the proposed Conference. The armaments in progress in his country are designed to meet attack from either Russians or English; but he considers the latter his best friends, and is willing to co-operate in any scheme for the integrity of the North-Western frontier. He will not accept dictation." From "the latter, his best friends," he receives a subsidy of one hundred and twenty thousand pounds a year!

It is interesting that the first Christian missionary to the Afghans was a converted Jew, Joseph Wolff, an eccentric man, who, more than sixty years ago, found his way alone from Armenia to Hindustan, through the almost unknown regions of Central Asia, preaching Christ as he went. "His journals," writes a missionary on the northern frontier, "are remarkable productions; some of his statements are startling to sober minds; but when read on the frontier of Northern India, with an intimate knowledge of the state and condition of the countries through which he journeyed, the romance of Joseph Wolff's travels becomes less romantic, and more real and life-like." At the mountain capital, Cabul, he discussed with a Muhammadan Moulvie in the presence of the once-famous Amir, Dost Mahommet Khan.

Afghanistan beyond the frontier has not been, so far as I know, accessible for regular missionary work. Independently of Mussulman fanaticism, an Englishman there, missionary or other, would be looked on with deep suspicion, not unnaturally. Have not the British often tried to bag that game? No wonder it is shy. I knew a man who, as a Christian "faquir," travelled through the Afghan country, and all the time he had an uncomfortable feeling that he was watched and followed, and did not feel his head safe on his shoulders. He noticed the same figures, with muffled face and downcast, but observant eyes, passing and repassing him many times on the road. He reached the gates of the Capital, and there was stopped, and finally, by order of the Amir, he was escorted back to the frontier, and dismissed into British territory.

The agents of the Church Missionary Society are as able and devoted a body of Christian workers as any in India, and they are in every part of the land. Two years before the Mutiny, this Society established a Mission to the Afghans, at Peshawar, the British frontier town, not many miles from the jaws of the Khyber Pass. The city is a bigoted Mussulman stronghold, and some apprehended danger from the preaching of the gospel in such a place. The Commissioner of the Division at that time was Sir Herbert Edwardes, a brave man and a wise ruler. From him the Mission received much sympathy and aid, for he was not one who believed that the preaching of the gospel would endanger British rule in India. Though his predecessor had fallen by the hand of an assassin, he fearlessly and openly expressed his determination, as civil ruler, to protect alike the Brahman priest, the Muhammadan teacher, and the Christian missionary. "And God honoured that Christian ruler in that very place, for he it was who, in the terrible mutiny of 1857, held the bigoted Muhammadans of the Trans-Indus territory with a firm hand, and made loyal soldiers of Afghan levies."

There is something pleasing and hopeful in the

A GROUP OF SIKHS.

following words of a Peshawar missionary: "I attach great importance to itineracy among the villages, which are beyond the corrupting influence of a large city and a large military cantonment. The farther I go from Peshawar, the more kindly am I received by the people. When in the Afghan villages, many are the delightful meetings which I have had, when Nicodemuses have come by night for fear of the people, to learn something of Christian teaching. The Afghan villagers are a very sociable class of men. Hospitality is the bond of perfectness to the Afghan mind." In the city a Christian congregation has been gathered, and hundreds of children are instructed in the schools of the Mission.

The history of this perilous outpost of missionary work cannot but excite the sympathy of Christian hearts. When the words quoted above were spoken, sixteen missionaries and eight missionaries' wives had been located at Peshawar within sixteen years, and of these, six had died at the station; one of them, the gifted Isidore Loewenthal, of the Presbyterian Mission, was shot by his servant a few months after completing and publishing the translation of the New Testament into the Pushtu language; two others had died in England, and seven had been compelled to relinquish the work through failure of health.

Another striking figure seen at times in the Capital is the Sikh from the land of the five rivers. Occasionally our Sikh soldiers are to be seen on the roads about Fort William, and the Maidan is dotted with their white tents. They are tall, stately men, hereditary warriors, whose prowess in the field has been proved both as our friends and our foes. "I'll tell you what I have seen," said an old English officer to me, "I have seen English troops in full flight before Sikhs on the battle-field." That was, I think, in the bloody struggle at Chillianwallah, when the English general at nightfall, having gained a victory that was nearly a defeat, withdrew from the field with a loss of 2,357 men and 89 officers in killed and wounded, judging he could not hold the ground if attacked by the Sikhs during the night. Soon after, the power of the Sikhs was broken. The wreck of their army submitted to an unconditional surrender, and laid down their arms at the feet of the English commander. Shere Singh, history tells us, set the example by delivering up his sword. Then the brave Sikh soldiers one by one passed by, casting their arms upon the heap, some in silent grief and tears, some with passionate exclamations. Not as cowards, but as brave men, they made a genuine submission to a power they could not resist; and since then, in trying times, they have shown themselves faithful friends to the British Government. Writing as a missionary, I do not hesitate to set these things down, for it is important, I think, that those in this land who support mission work should know the qualities and the story of the races we have to do with in India.

The Sikhs afford an instance of a nation growing out of a religious reform. There are two names specially venerated among them. Nanuk, the founder of the religion, was the son of a petty village trader, and was born in 1469, in a village near the ancient city of Lahore. He was tolerant, philosophic, devout, desirous of knowing God, and of growing inwardly pure. The errors of Hinduism, idol-worship, caste, the immolation of widows, he rejected. For himself and his followers he sought freedom from mental and spiritual bondage. The sect grew in numbers, but had no political significance until bitter persecution at the hands of the Muhammadans made them mortal foes to the Mussulman rule, and changed peaceable religionists into warriors and marauders.

Govindo, the other leader of special memory, was the tenth guru from the founder of the sect. His father had been imprisoned and put to death by order of the bigoted Emperor Aurungzebe. Burning with a sense of injustice, he armed his followers, and led them against the Muhammadans; but his troops were scattered, his children put to death, and he himself wandered a hopeless exile, bereft at times of reason, and was at last assassinated. After these reverses, the Sikhs betook themselves to the mountains north of the Punjab, sometimes issuing forth with fire and sword, and making terrible reprisals. Finally, in the decline of the Moghul dynasty, they established themselves an independent and powerful nation, with an hereditary hatred of Muhammadans.

To the American Presbyterians belongs the honour of commencing, in 1834, missionary work among the Sikhs. They have been followed by many other societies. The Punjab, after a long experience of disturbance, and the calamities and changing fortunes of war, was annexed by the British in 1849. Since then it has become "as a field which the Lord hath blessed;" civil officers of high ability have ruled the province, missionaries of marked talent and thorough consecration have laboured for the moral and spiritual good of

THE TEMPLE OF AMRITSAR.

the people The numerical results of mission work are seen in a native Christian community of about eighteen thousand, and in Mission schools, in which nineteen thousand of the young are instructed.

In the history of mission work among the Sikhs there is an incident which carries us back to the Mutiny of 1857. When Delhi was in the hands of the mutineers, among our native troops was a regiment of Sikhs, the 24th Punjab Infantry, who had been enlisted in that time of our great exigency, and had proved themselves good soldiers. They found in Delhi, among the prizes of war, a number of Christian books, and felt a desire to understand their contents. Through the study of these, in which they were helped by missionaries and others, many of them became Christians. A devout officer allowed them to go to him for instruction, and held, on Sundays, a service which was attended by a good number of the men, and several native officers. About forty persons received baptism. The Government, hearing of this movement, became concerned, and a despatch was sent forbidding officers to use their influence to turn native soldiers from their own religion. By this, it seems, the spirit of inquiry was chilled and the movement checked.

Thirty-one years ago, 1862, a general Missionary Conference was held at the ancient city, Lahore. It must have been an interesting moment when the chairman of the assembly rose and said " he felt sure that the members of the Conference would rejoice with himself in seeing among them the Rajah of Kapurthala (a Punjabi prince); and he begged to introduce him and his brother, the Sirdar Bikrama

Singh, to the Conference." Twelve years after, this same brother was baptized by a native preacher of the Presbyterian Mission.

In my first chapter I dealt with the prospects of Christianity in India. Since writing the preceding pages, I have seen the Statistical Tables of Indian Missions, published in 1892 with the authority of the Calcutta Missionary Conference, giving the numerical progress of Missions during nine years, 1881–90. The compilers anticipate that considerable disappointment will be felt at these results. Doubtless many, like myself, have awaited, with great interest, the appearance of these tables, wondering whether, in regard to Bengal, for instance, "the enormous increase of 64 per cent." in the native Christian population of that province during the preceding decade would be repeated in the ten years closing with 1891. We could not but desire, and even hope, that the possibility suggested by Sir W. W. Hunter, though his words were carefully and wisely guarded, might become a reality.

"All I can say is, that if the native Christian population is increasing 64 per cent. during these ten years, it will be one of the most wonderful triumphs which Christianity has had in the world."[1] The tables show that Bengal has had an increase of 30 per cent., less than half the progress realized in the previous decade; and for the whole of India, with Ceylon and Burmah, the increase has been 34 per cent. in nine years. Some good men, on the basis of statistics, have calculated the number of years required for the conversion

[1] See page 19.

of the whole of India; but experience teaches us the unreliableness of these calculations. The Christian movement may be hindered or accelerated in ways we cannot foresee.

The more we know of India, the better do we understand the tremendous difficulties in the way of its conversion to the religion of Christ. Far removed from the healthy stir and activities of western nations, India, in deep loneliness, has developed a religion and philosophy peculiarly her own, and a mighty system has been consolidating during thousands of years of undisturbed isolation. Missionaries, brought face to face daily with the difficulties of this great Christian enterprise, desire to be remembered, and are remembered, in the prayers of Christ's people. Since my return to England, I have been struck with the tone of some prayers offered in my hearing on behalf ot missionaries. They are, of course, prayed for as those who are labouring amidst discouragements, and without doubt there are great discouragements in all Christian work. But it seems to be thought—I judge from prayers I have listened to—that missionaries are carrying on work weighted with feelings of discouragement, depression, and even despondency. "That brother," I have sometimes thought, "either has little hope himself, or judges that missionaries are working with little hope."

But what, in truth, are the feelings of missionaries? I have known many of them, and in all varieties of the circumstances peculiar to their life. I have visited them at their stations, northward at the foot of the Snowy Mountains, southward under the burning equator, in busy cities, and on quiet plains. I have been in their chapels, schools, and villages, and this one thing has been impressed on my mind, that missionaries are a cheerful, hopeful, happy class of workers. Of course there are varieties of temperament among them—there are optimists and pessimists; but speaking of them generally, I should be surprised indeed if any sympathetic soul who has visited them could say he found them a dejected class of men. We may thank God for the confidence, hopefulness, and buoyancy which characterise our brethren in the Mission field.